Blog

I0014866

Table of Contents

Introduction

Welcome dear prospective bloggers. I don't. No one does. However, that is not the point. I haven't earned a huge number of dollars from blogging to lecture you about it, yet I can unhesitatingly say I have accomplished something not very many individuals in the blogging circle have done, and that is I've bombed various occasions at blogging. I have contributed and lost cash attempting various approaches to show signs of improvement at it. So for what reason would you need to peruse a book composed by somebody who has committed a great deal of errors in the first place? Think of me as your companion who needs you to improve. Will my techniques in this book help you become an incredible blogger? Completely! Would you be able to arrive at a point where you can acquire enough cash from blogging and make it your essential wellspring of pay? Indeed, completely! These gestures are expecting you have the persistence and are happy to place in the work. I will direct you through everything. Simply don't expect it won't agree with any exertion from your stance.

I would prefer not to overpower you with data, so I separated the book into two sections. The initial segment will enable you to begin, give you a push away from any detectable hindrance waters, while the subsequent part will enable you to endure the tempests, the quiets and the creatures. Of the two sections, the initial segment is meant to kick you off by helping you set up the site, compose substance and keep a relentless substance stream, all of which falls under the customary blogging range.

The subsequent part centers on the cutting edge standards of blogging. Blogging isn't normal any longer; you can't simply set up a site and hope to see ten thousand guests and furthermore have budgetary objectives verified it. Blogging is more extensive now, so the second piece of the book concentrates decisively on that. It reveals insight into a blog being an outlet of significant worth, which can be deciphered by a hundred various ways.

You have all that you need directly here, don't surge it, adhere to the guidelines and tips tenaciously, have tolerance, and you'll be a superior blogger before the finish of the book. Things being what they are, will we move?

As talked about before, I will initially direct you through setting up an essential site for the blog, composing and keeping up a relentless progression of substance. When we set up this, we can plunge a lot more profound into extending the blog.

The initial segment includes a few sub-parts. To begin with, I'll talk about blogging misinterpretations you may have. I'd likewise prefer to discuss key belief systems you have to comprehend in the event that you need to be an extraordinary blogger. At that point we'll plunge into the specialized part, where I will control you on how you can set up the site and start making content. Try not to stress over the details! I will disentangle everything for you so you need not have a specialized foundation to comprehend the means.

So how about we center on the initial segment and prepare our blog up and yet before that, you'll have to know the key belief systems.

Fundamental Thoughts and clearing

Misconceptions

As a writer, individuals blame me for transforming mundane innovative subjects into philosophical stories, and I'll accept that as a compliment. I genuinely accept there are a million different ways to succeed at anything, as long as you have your rudiments secured. So indeed, I am going to talk nuts and bolts, and on the other hand that you need to prevail about blogging or whatever else so far as that is concerned, build up a stomach for learning the essentials. Understanding the establishment enables you to form everything as indicated by your vision. I realize you'd love to get straightforwardly to the arrangement procedure, however these ideas are basic for you to get it. So have tolerance and experience these completely. These philosophies will help you build up a mindset for blogging that is important for the since quite a while ago run. Let's start.

Value is Vital

One of the primary reasons you are perusing this book is on the grounds that you need to begin as a blogger, and not just that, you need to gain cash out of it. That is fine. I am not making a decision about you. Cash is indispensable to satisfying our everyday needs. The issue, be that as it may, is in profiting the prime explanation that you are blogging.

Ideally, you'd continue blogging and not stress over regularly making a dime in light of your affection for the game. Tragically however, life isn't so impeccable. Truly, you need to profit from your blog at some phase to continue your way of life while as yet seeking after your opportunity to express. The speediest route not to profit from blogging is to pursue it, pursuing is the driving reason for why practically 80% of individuals can't support blogging and quit. So I am letting you know not to pursue the cash, and yet I state that your blog will require to make benefit at some stage. Can get befuddling, so let me give you a model:

Suppose I am a photography fan and I compose a blog on the equivalent. You are investigating the flawless waters of photography, and you discover my blog. You appear to like what I compose, so you buy in to it. I expound on my different encounters in photography including the errors I've made, which I need individuals like you to evade, the positives I've increased through my voyage also, considerably more. Presently, as a novice, you discover my blog creative, thus now, I am giving you esteem and anticipating nothing consequently. Presently a half year has passed, I keep making substance and individuals like you continue devouring it. The persistent worth that I am giving my group of spectators has made them trust me and my sentiments.

Suppose I compose a post titled 'The Best Camera Equipment for Beginners' and rundown the majority of my prescribed items. Presently, for a learner, my suggestion is a higher priority than a TV business in light of the fact that not at all like the TVC, I am consistently offering some benefit. I have connected all the items in my post so you can get to them rapidly. I have partner joins (more on this later) which when tapped on and made a buy from, get me a commission.

So as you pursue my blog, you read the article, and in the event that you are intending to put resources into a few gear, you look for a similar utilizing the connections I've referenced, and subsequently I get a commission. Pause! I am not inducing you to purchase the gear here. I am suggesting it, and it is a legit suggestion from years or long periods of involvement in this field. I am not a sales rep. I am a guide. The subsidiary connections produce a commission that causes me bolsters the blog and my way of life so I can keep on offering an unprejudiced worth.

The above model demonstrates that regardless of what the online world figures, you will consistently have approaches to profit from blogging. You should concentrate on offering some benefit and not on profiting, and everything else will become alright.

In an online world, where a profile of a wonderful lady could take care of business in his 50s, trust is the hardest to acquire. Furthermore, how can one get this tricky trust? Blogging is a marathon, not a dash. On the other hand that you need to blog to make sure you can purchase the following iPhone at that point I am sorry to learn you, blogging isn't for you. On the other hand that your solitary point is to purchase the following iPhone, you'll take alternate routes and not concentrate on offering some incentive. Regardless of whether you acquire enough cash to purchase an iPhone, it'll all end when your crowd loses their trust towards you. Thinking present moment, particularly in the field of blogging, will prompt disappointment.

I can truly make $500 in a month from blogging on the most arbitrary point; however I won't be ready to make another dime of it in the coming months. When individuals realize I am only one of those advertisers looking for their cash, they'd need no piece of me. So it's smarter to make $100 every month for the following year than make $500 in the primary month and nothing a while later.

In this universe of blogging, esteem sits central. The more worth you give, the more group of spectators you get and the more group of spectators you get, the more ways you need to profit. Try not to pursue the cash. Hope to offer some benefit and everything else will pursue.

The Prompt Satisfaction Virus

I need to go over this point pretty much every time I am discussing imaginative work, yet I'd preferably go over it and be dull than not utter a word. So I don't get my meaning by Instant Gratification? What's more, for what reason am I talking about this in a book that spotlights on blogging? All things considered, you'll find your solutions as you read further. First however, time for certain inquiries.

Do you recollect the last time you requested something on the web? A cell phone, a couple of shoes, anything? Obviously you recollect, and I will wager you have purchased something from an online store in the previous 20-30 days, am I right? Another inquiry, when was the last time you requested nourishment on the web or by means of telephone? Once more, odds are, you have done this as of late. Some time ago I used to peruse the paper before anything else, not to get the most recent news yet to peruse what's on TV for that day and if there was an extraordinary film I could watch, I would take note of the planning and the channel number on my little scratch pad. Presently times are extraordinary. We have Video on Demand administrations, for example, Netflix, Amazon Prime Video and so on where you can marathon watch the whole period of your preferred TV arrangement while tasting Chocolate Milk at 3 am.

Every one of these extravagances has made our lives far increasingly agreeable, and I am grateful for it, yet it has likewise made us purposely or something else, inclined to Instant Gratification. We apply this hypothesis of Instantaneousness to pretty much every situation and expect everything to happen rapidly. It gets unsafe when a similar conduct is reflected in work, family or other significant issues.

Presently individuals have a lesser tolerance for relationships, and they are happy to separate after the tiniest of quarrels. Individuals at work raise stopping when something sudden or heartbreaking occurs. We as a whole have intentionally or accidentally become upset, a tad at once.

I am not accusing the innovation here. All things considered, I am arriving at your eyes due to the extraordinary headways of innovation. We need mindfulness, that's it in a nutshell. Our folks, grandparents have preferred tolerance over us, they didn't have these cutting edge interruptions, be that as it may, we do, and you recognize what, we can't sit and whimper about it.

As you start your blogging venture, you will experience a dismal truth: You won't hit a million supporters at any point in the near future, and you'll have a great deal to state however not very many ready to tune in. Here is the place you don't become irritated and continue creating content.

In the event that you put the time and exertion into it, you'll be a fruitful blogger in whatever theme you pick, in any case, it won't come immediately, and I'd like you to have a mentality that supports this idea.

Can you make a sustainable Income from your Blog?

The long answer is yes. What's more, no, there is no short answer here. For what reason isn't there a fast answer? Since that is unequivocally what you need to hear. Have you at any point made a 'How-to' Google search or on the other hand a YouTube search recently, for example, 'how to make a YouTube video' or 'how to make a sandwich'? On the other hand that you have, you'll regularly see a 'quick' proposal popping. 'Instructions to get more supporters for Instagram Fast', or 'how to get more devotees on Twitter Fast', these individuals need to make a Sandwich quick also. On the other hand that it were up to them, they wouldn't flame broil a Grilled Sandwich to make it quick.

In the event that I state truly, you can make blogging your essential wellspring of salary. Some of you may accept it as a prompt yes and quit everything and start blogging. This fervor, however, would fall off the edge in the main month itself when you make nada out of your blog.

I'll ask you something. Would you be able to bring home the bacon out of selling Sweets?

Take as much time as is needed and think about the potential situations here. The direct answer is no, and the long answer is yes. On the other hand that you are extraordinary at making desserts and you cherish making desserts for individuals, you can make in excess of a living out of it. You'll have the tolerance and the drive important to go through the hardest time of any business, which is, most likely, the beginning. The equivalent goes for blogging; If you blog about something that you adore, no adjustment on the planet can prevent you from arriving at incredible statures. The market may change, web based life may, yet you will adjust. To start with, however, you should experience this time of battle where you find out about your expertise in the subject and become familiar with crowds. When you experience these encounters, you become articulate about where precisely you need to concentrate your vitality on. This isn't an ideal opportunity to go all genuine on blogging. This is the ideal opportunity for experimentation and experience. My answer remains yes. You can make a feasible salary from blogging so stop agonizing over the outcome and spotlight on the procedure. Plunge your toes, change themes, figure what you adore, commit heaps of errors, and gain from them.

Trust me when I state there are a million different ways to profit from your blog, and you can make a great deal of cash yet right now toward the beginning, you should concentrate on offering some benefit from your Content, everything else will occur.

Misconceptions about Blogging

I've invested a great deal of energy discussing the outlook required to be a fruitful blogger. Presently I might want to examine a few misguided judgments you may have. We regularly fabricate confusions from a separation, with an absence of learning for the subject.

The main misguided judgment individuals have is that blogging is income sans work. Here's a reality: All the genuine methods for causing cash to require diligent work, however you get the chance to pick your toxic substance. At the point when you work in a field you cherish, the diligent work doesn't appear to be so difficult any longer. What's more, that is the reason energetic bloggers profit, they cherish what they do, and that makes them put forward quite a lot more exertion, which at that point receives awesome benefits.

Let's assume you are an astounding nursery worker who makes about $500 a month taking a shot at a land that spreads for a fourth of a section of land. Hearing the stories of your ability, a rich individual extends to you an employment opportunity to chip away at his one-section of land garden, while multiplying your present pay, will you accept the position? Most presumably you will, and in view of the cash as well as for the love of planting. Chipping away at just about multiple times your present region is a test, yet your enthusiasm for the field makes you need to acknowledge this demand. You realize your outstanding task at hand will increment, yet it is to a greater degree a rush for you than an errand. A similar activity may sound hard for somebody who isn't infatuated with cultivating as you seem to be.

It requires exertion to prevail in any field yet picking something that you cherish makes the work sense that play than work itself. It makes you put in substantially more exertion, which when met with consistency, gets you to greatness.

So truly, blogging will require work, tolerance, and determination, however when you pick the privilege point to blog, each procedure will get simpler. The explanation you need to blog shouldn't be on the grounds that you figure you should work less to procure all the more however about working at the perfect spot, so independent of the amount you procure, your work never feels like a task. So no, blogging isn't pain free income except if you blog about a point you cherish.

Setting up a Blog requires technical knowledge

No, you don't. Possibly 10 years prior it would have been an alternate answer however now it is truly straightforward for anybody to begin a blog and look after it, with next to zero specialized information.

Presently, we have apparatuses and administrations that deal with the specialized part while we center on the plan part. Prior, you'd need to contract a Website engineer to construct a site for your blog and afterward rely upon them to keep up it while failing to have a lot of command over it. Presently, however, you can actually set up and structure your site in under a day. These devices and administrations have a slight expectation to learn and adapt however, yet you'll get around it when you use them.

After you read the accompanying entry, you may blame me for being sermonizing, yet I will acknowledge the misleading allegations on the other hand that it causes you set up a decent establishment. Prior, I revealed to you that the best approach to pick up your group of spectators' trust is to offer them incredible worth, yet I never revealed to you how. Well at that point, we should begin! How can one give incredible worth?

Extraordinary worth originates from a fair articulation. Truly, one more worldview to the effectively huge confound, remain with me however, this is the remainder of the ideas you have to get it. Nothing more, I guarantee.

As a blogger and substance maker, one of the most continuous inquiries individual bloggers pose to me is "Vikrant, I am an apprentice blogger/you tuber/content maker, how would I stand apart from the swarm, the online world is loaded with individuals like me, what would i be able to do to stick out and make my own personality?" My answer is a two-word presentation "Act naturally". When I offer individuals this response, I normally get a gesture yet not a persuading one, as though individuals might suspect I will give them a perplexing recipe to stand apart from the group. In the event that you solicit any from the incredible substance makers, they will give you the same answer. So how does acting naturally bring about standing apart from the group? Here's the secret:

In this universe of 7.7 billion individuals, every one of us is distinctive in light of the fact that we have experienced our remarkable arrangement of encounters that have molded us to be what our identity is. You may have had an completely unexpected childhood in comparison to me. You may have had a harder adolescence than other individuals, you may have invested more energy in the town than the city, I may love the city more than the town, and another person may appreciate the field more. We're all unique, and henceforth we've just stood apart from the group; it's only a point of fair articulation. The majority of your encounters to date have formed your feelings towards nearly everything, and when you express these, you normally stand apart from the group.

I'll give you my model: When I began composing articles, blog entries, I read a great deal about how I could make them sound impeccable to the peruse and appear to be an expert. I attempted different genius methods, began utilizing more extravagant words, increasingly formal tone, and so on. When I composed my first eBook on a cell phone guide in

2014, it resembled a textbook, all proper language, no exchanges, no mockery. Maybe I had been compelled to compose it. It had my name on it, however it wasn't me. The book had normal deals, yet some way or another I was upset about it. I realized it wasn't me.

Possibly I needed to seem like a Pro too-aesthetic to-utilize mockery sort of writer. I am a cheerful individual, and I want to joke around constantly, however none of it reflected in the book.

The theme of the book was specialized, yet at the same time, it didn't have my stamp on it! So after around about fourteen days from the hour of the underlying discharge, I unpublished the book, took out an old notebook, my preferred dark pen and began composing. Not a consideration for the sentence structure, structure or composition. I was composing the book as though I am having a discussion with the peruse, and I needed the peruse to realize this is me. If they somehow managed to meet me on an arbitrary road by one way or another, I would sound simply as I did in the books. Following two weeks, I composed the book in my bona fide style and distributed it.

I couldn't have cared less about sales, feedback or anything. I simply needed a veritable adaptation of me in the book, regardless of if individuals got it or didn't. Truly, the book did affirm, I got a lot of positive feedback, however there was something I learned through that voyage, 'Acting naturally is a definitive street to independence and hanging out in an inventive field, regardless of whether that be moving, drawing, blogging, podcasting or anything'.

Truly, I realize my books do not have the wonderful language structure, sentence structure and substantially more of the conventional books yet you recognize what, I couldn't care less, I have acknowledged myself and my composition style. I would prefer not to be the instructor who encourages a class loaded with uninterested individuals, drawing irregular figures on the writing board. Rather, I need to be the coach who sits adjacent to you, tastes a couple runs of your espresso, and demonstrates to you what I've realized through my missteps.

So till right up 'til today, I haven't changed my composition style, I look for discussions with the pursuer, a little giggle to a great extent and if in this procedure you discover some new information, I couldn't be more joyful!

This doesn't mean I am a complete Snob and won't engage a chance to improve myself. I can get the book composed by a Ghostwriter yet it won't be me, and I can't take that. On the other hand that a Million individuals read my book tomorrow and just one of them was to like it, I would love it since I give that one individual enormous incentive through my work and that as well, in my true style.

I need the equivalent for you. I need you to express your heart out without agonizing over judgment. Your blog is yours, and there is no point attempting to seem like another person. Possibilities are, the individual you are attempting to duplicate is famous in light of their fair suppositions and the bona fide style to express those conclusions.

It doesn't make a difference on the other hand that you have zero or a thousand devotees, you can at present contend with the most settled of bloggers, your bit of leeway is you, and don't you ever set out remove it by difficult to be one of them.

What to search for a Blog?

I know the philosopher in me can get a piece diverted now and again, however it was important to tell you about the key philosophies that will enable you to be a superior substance maker. Presently we get to the execution part. Before you put whenever or cash into the blogging forms, you need to choose what you need to blog about. I have a brisk errand for you which won't take over five minutes. Take a pen and a paper furthermore, record a rundown of things you cherish or are energetic about. This is conceptualizing so don't think a lot. Likewise, the length of your rundown isn't significant, your rundown can contain a solitary thing or twenty, I am not judging.

Is it accurate to say that you are finished? Take as much time as is needed on the other hand that you need to, however finish this errand. On the other hand that it weren't vital; I wouldn't have requested your five minutes. When you are done, select the main three things that you completely love. If I somehow managed to conceptualize a comparative show, it will look something like this:

- Gardening
- Playing the Guitar
- Reading
- Watching Movies
- Singing
- Writing short stories
- Tennis
- Photography

In my rundown, there are a couple of things that I cherish accomplishing more than others, I play the Guitar much superior to I yard my grass. I adore photography more than I cherish Singing.

Once more, this is for individuals who have a greater rundown. On the other hand that you had three things or less in your rundown to start with, at that point it's extraordinary, you have a sifted rundown as of now. Keep the rundown for what it's worth. Presently for the best three rundown things, on the other hand that you have a more prominent affinity towards a solitary one, at that point no issue, pick it. On the other hand that you have equivalent enthusiasm towards every one of them, at that point select any. The chose thing is presently what you will blog about. How about we jump deeper?

Starting a Blog

A blog is a website, and we have to assemble this website before we start with content. I will show both of you strategies to construct a website for your blog. The first is the 'Free Method', where you can get to know utilizing a website, composing content, and so forth. This technique is just to get your feet wet; on the other hand that you need to swim the untamed waters of blogging, you should utilize the second technique, the 'Paid Method'.

Peruse both the strategies and after that choose. In the event that you are new to blogging, I recommend you actualize the 'Free strategy', get to know composing a blog and after that when you're prepared, actualize the 'Paid strategy'. Your blog potential will never be acknowledged utilizing the 'Free technique', so the change to the 'Paid Method' is impending. So on the other hand that you need to quit fooling around with blogging right away; at that point actualize the 'Paid technique'.

The Free Method

This strategy is basic and includes no specialized gibberish. The Internet has favored us with a couple of online administrations that help us set up a free website. These administrations deal with the specialized part, while we center on the structure part. The following are the best three website building administrations:

Wix.com

WordPress.com

Blogger.com

We will manufacture our website utilizing Wix.com in light of the fact that it takes into account extraordinary usefulness for nothing clients. Pursue the means underneath to make a free website on Wix.

Wix Walkthrough

Go to 'www.wix.com' and adhere to the underneath guidelines to make a free blog:

Stage 1: Go to www.wix.com: On the landing page, click on 'Begin', checked red in the picture underneath:

Stage 2: Once you click on begin; you will get a login page. Presently we can't login in light of the fact that we haven't made a record yet.

Stage 3: On the following page, fill in the subtleties and snap on 'sign up':

Stage 4: On the following page, click on 'skip'. At that point on the following page, we'll be designing our blog utilizing a design layout, so click on 'pick a format':

Step 5: The next page is the Design template page. Here, Wix offers a plethora of beautiful web designs. From personal blogs to e-commerce sites, you'll see everything here. On the left hand side are the design categories (marked blue) and on the correct hand side and the templates (marked red). Presently click on the Blogs and Forums category (marked green):

Step 6: Now you'll just see the design templates specific for blogs. Presently discover design templates that match your blog niche. On the other hand that you hover over a design template, you get two alternatives, either to 'view' or to 'edit'. Feel free to tap on view, presently you'll see a full page design preview of the template. Keep exploring these templates and when you locate the one you like, click on 'edit':

Designing your blog using Wix

When you discover the template you like, then you click on 'edit'. It then takes you to the Wix editor, which may take some time to stack. Once it's loaded, designing the blog becomes really simple. Wix has great walkthrough videos on the best way to edit these design templates, create posts, and include online networking symbols and significantly more. You can discover the videos here.

The videos on the above connection will help you establish your blog. However, we have created a free blog on Wix, it doesn't have an area name (more on this later) i.e. our own blog address, furthermore, has numerous confinements. Presently let me introduce the 'Paid Method'.

Like I've stated, the progress to the paid method is necessary however that doesn't mean you have to do it immediately. Take your time, get acquainted with blogging, and when you are ready to invest money, implement the method I am going to tell you.

The Paid Method

The videos on the above connection will help you establish your blog. However, we have created a free blog on Wix, it doesn't have an area name (more on this later) i.e. our very own blog address, furthermore, has numerous confinements. Presently let me introduce the 'Paid Method'. Like I've stated, the progress to the paid method is necessary however that doesn't mean you have to do it immediately. Take your time, get acquainted with blogging, and when you are ready to invest money, implement the method I am going to tell you.

Building a website utilizing the Paid method involves three simple steps:

1) Choosing a domain name

2) Choosing a Hosting service

3) Designing the blog utilizing a Word Press theme.

I couldn't imagine anything better than to give you a one-fits-all set up guide that launches your blog without a need to get into the technicalities. Unfortunately I can't. This book is meant for an international audience and space name or facilitating companies implement different estimating and feature structure based on a specific nation. A space name or a facilitating plan offered in my nation may not be available for yours or vice versa. The exact opposite thing I need for you is uncertainty in the process of setting up a website for your blog.

So I have devised a set of directions for the above steps that are universal and are simple to understand also. Experience the steps below and your website will up and running in no time.

Step 1: Choosing a Domain Name:

Presently, there will be some technicalities and a few new terms, yet I am here to rearrange everything for you.

Area names are unique web addresses that direct the guest to the desired website. When you type in 'google.com' in your browser, you generally reach Google's homepage. Did you ever wonder for what reason does that happen? Well, Google has purchased the area name 'google.com' from a space name registrar, and that is the reason every time someone types in 'www.google.com' on a browser, the guest is directed towards the Google website.

We have to do likewise for our blog, and I state it is our own because I believe we are in this together. Our blog needs a unique address a.k.a. area name, so first, let's figure out what we are going to call it.

I can't choose your space name for you because it depends on the theme of your blog. A blog that focuses on Politics shouldn't have a space name 'atozrecipes.com'; it ought to rather be called something like 'theopinion.com'. So you'll have to decide the area name for our blog, however I'll help you make a better decision. Take a pen and paper; conceptualize possible area names for our blog. Here are some tips for the same:

1. Maintain a strategic distance from long area names; target something between 7-15 words.

2. The better it is to pronounce, the easier it is to recommend to people.

3. Make it relevant to your niche.

4. You can't put a space between an area names. You can insert special characters, for example,

'@,*, _,- ', however it is advised to stay away from them. So make sure the space name looks pleasant altogether without spaces.

E.g., on the other hand that I need to begin a blog that revolves around traveling, my possible area names list would look something like this:

- *Cluelesstraveller.com*

- *Wrongdirection.com*

- *Beentheredonethat.com*

- *howdidIgethere.com*

- *wholesometraveller.com*

- *thetraveladdict.com*

- *TheAnxiousTraveller.com*

- *Takemeplaces.com*

Presently the above is a conceptualize rundown, and your rundown can be longer or shorter, doesn't matter. In the event that you notice however, there is a trace of cheesy banter in the majority of the names that is because the niche is lighthearted and by nature, I am cheesy, so why not reflect both in the area name.

The tone of the blog is your voice, and it ought to reflect in your area name. A blog called 'wry movie reviews' ought to have a mocking tone to its posts and a relevant area name.

Before you finalize a space name, you should run your potential rundown by an area name registrar. As space names are unique, chances are, some of the names that you've shortlisted have already been taken by someone else.

As should be obvious above, my quest for the area name 'justastupidblog.com' can be fulfilled as it is available. Likewise, as should be obvious in the area marked red, hostgator is suggesting space name extensions like '.host', '.net', '.club' and '.data'. We needn't bother with any of those; we just need the '.com' extension.

Go to any of the accompanying websites below and run your rundown of potential area names:

- www.hostgator.com/areas
- www.gogaddy.com/areas
- www.domain.com

For the present, simply run your rundown through the above websites; don't make a purchase at the present time.

Remember, we need a '.com.' extension to our space name, in the event that it isn't available, area name providers often give you an alternative to use a '.net', '.website' or some other extensions for the same name. Try not to purchase those by any stretch of the imagination. It is tempting as these providers do offer them at a discounted price, yet that is because nobody gets them in any case.

Domain Privacy Production

Area name registrars offer an extra feature with a space registration ordinarily called as 'Privacy Protection'. So what's going on here? What's more, do you need it? Well, let me give you a foundation of its cause.

When websites were introduced to the world, it was required that the space name details counting the owner details be made open. This was made for general people to discover the details of an accountable person for a website. It was altogether made in a decent soul, yet it has become quite an issue now. There are two primary problems with your space name details opening up to the world:

1. Identity Theft: The Internet is a double-edged sword, and there are consistently people attempting to use it for noxious activities, one such type of action is usually called as 'Identity Theft'. It is fundamentally a person extracting personal details of someone else and afterward utilizing these details to imitate the other person online. It may not sound that huge of a deal to you, however trust me, it is a lot bigger than you might suspect.

E.g. let's say I purchase a space name, and I don't sign up for a Privacy Protection program. Presently my space name details are visible to the world, including my home address, email address what's more, phone number. Imagine a scenario where a person takes those details finds a picture of me from my social Media profile and pretends to be me on some other website? What's more, imagine a scenario where they take it further by engaging in Hate Speech on sensitive subjects? The repercussions of these possibilities are alarming.

2. Infinite Spamming: As I mentioned in the point above, your personal details are open, this includes your email address and phone number. Plenty of companies that provide space name and hosting services search for the personal data of space names without Privacy Protection, and after that they call you for offers, send marketing advertisements on your email address etc.

So what would you be able to do? Well, you can either select into Privacy Protection or not stress by any means. Or on the other hand you can provide a less specific version of your personal details during the area name registration. The above picture demonstrates to you the choice to pick in for 'Privacy

Protection', you'll generally discover it ticked as a matter of course.

Once you have an area name you need and the '.com' extension available for it, here's something you need to know: When you purchase the area name and the hosting service (discussed in the next sub-chapter) from the same organization, it saves you from experiencing a bundle of technicalities. So I'd advise you to do likewise. On the other hand that you are checking the space name accessibility through Hostgator (hostgator.com/spaces), feel free to purchase the area name for a length of one year.

Hostgator isn't available in every one of the countries however, so on the other hand that it isn't available in your nation, go for Go Daddy (godaddy.com/areas). Make sure you purchase the area name for just a single year. Don't overcommit now as you might need to change it later. One year is the base length available so let it all out?

Notice: Please make sure you check the last price for your purchase; these service providers often select longer spans as default. They additionally tend to include the assessment later, which somewhat increases the last price.

Once your payment is successful, you'll receive an email from the space name provider with the receipt and the credentials for the Control Panel of your space name.

The email you will receive from the space registrar will have credentials as appeared in the above picture. Mind you, this is an email sent from my space name registrar, so your email may appear to be unique.

Step 2: Choosing a Hosting

Area names are addresses, you've gotten yourself an address on the Internet however what about the house? Websites require numerous files which include texts, images, music and significantly more. Whenever you visit a website, everything you see is stored on a computer somewhere. Your space name purchase doesn't include files storage, for this, you need to discover a hosting provider, which will host your files.

These hosting providers have numerous computers running 24x7 and for a predefined fee, they provide you with access to store all your blog files on their computers.

Some of you may state, for what reason wouldn't i be able to simply put every one of those blog files without anyone else computer? Well, that is a great question however will your personal computer remain on 24x7? People all around the globe will attempt to access your blog, and every time they do, your computer must be connected to the Internet for them to experience the contents of your blog.

Even on the other hand that you decided to keep your computer connected to the Internet while hosting your blog files 24x7, your low Internet speeds would make the blog load gradually, an nobody needs to visit a blog that takes quite a while to stack. So looking back, you do need a host. Try not to stress.

Hosting services start as low as $5 per month. Hosting providers can and will attempt to confuse you, so absent a lot of technical gobbled book, here's what you should choose:

Below is a rundown of the most well-known hosting services on the planet. However, to sidestep the greater part of the technicalities, make sure your Hosting service and space name registrar are the same. So in the event that you purchased your space name from Hostgator, choose the same for your Hosting. Same for Go Daddy!

- www.hostgator.com/wordpress-hosting
- www.godaddy.com/hosting/wordpress-hosting
- www.bluehost.com/wordpress/wordpress-hosting

We need to get a 'Word Press Hosting' plan for our blog. When you click on the above connections, you will be taken to the Word Press Hosting page. There you will be presented with different plans. Like what you see in the below screenshot.

We are simply beginning our blog so we needn't bother with a resourceful hosting plan for the present, so choose the most fundamental arrangement you can discover. In the above example, the most essential arrangement is the 'Starter' plan, which comes with more than enough resources for our blog.

The above screenshot is for Hostgator, in the event that you are on Go Daddy, use the same criteria. Discover the most essential arrangement of the part and choose it yet make sure you are on the 'Word Press Hosting' page.

The length of the hosting affects the price, the longer the term, the lower the price. The price displayed is often for prolonged lengths, for example, three years or five years, yet when you click on the drop-down catch, you get to realize the shorter length costs. I advise you to go for a multi month span period, which gives you enough leverage to upgrade or even change the hosting plan later.

Once your payment for the hosting services is made, you'll be prompted to create a username what's more, secret phrase for your Word Press administrator page. Create it and afterward proceed. Likewise, remember to keep these Word Press credentials convenient, as we'll need them to update our blog.

Presently, you've registered a space name and your Word Press hosting is up and running. We presently need to connect the area name to the Word Press hosting. To do this, essentially call the

Customer support number of your hosting service and tell them you'd like to interface the two, and they'll do it for you. On the other hand that you encounter any problems in the above process, call the hosting service customer support or reach out to me. In the event that somehow you've ended purchasing the area name and the hosting from different web service companies, click here for a detailed guide on setting up your blog.

Presently our blog is up and running yet we need to design it. Word Press as a stage is free, however the premium themes on Word Press aren't. However, until further notice, we don't need to invest in a premium theme. Free themes on Word Press are for the most part endorsement demos of premium themes, so you don't get a lot of usefulness in them. However, there is a free theme on Word Press called 'Shamrock', which is made for bloggers and offers a huge amount of features.

Designing the Blog: Installation

Installing Shamrock can be dubious for someone who hasn't used Word Press before. So below is a step-by-step guide on the most proficient method to introduce Shamrock on your website:

Step 1: Now we need to login to our Word Press administrator panel. For example, if my area name is 'www.tennisfnatic.com', then I need to enter 'www.tennisfnatic.com/wp-login'. Presently, you'll be prompted for the username and secret key, enter your Word Press administrator credentials.

Step 3: Now click on 'Appearance' and after that on 'Themes', as demonstrated as follows:

Step 4: Now click on 'Include New' and after that in the search bar, type 'Shamrock'. Then you'll see a result like the one displayed below. Presently click on 'Introduce' and after that on 'Activate'.

Presently you've authoritatively installed and activated the Shamrock Word Press theme on your website. Presently let's use it to design the blog.

Designing the Blog: Design

Designing the blog utilizing a Word Press theme can be dubious, so I've created a few walkthrough videos on the same, you can discover them here. Shamrock is a free Word Press theme. Its usefulness will support your needs until you need more freedom with your blog design. In the event that and when you feel the need to upgrade to a premium theme, I'd suggest you go for the 'Divi' theme. Its expenses $89 yet it is completely customizable.

Mind you, there is no need to invest in a Premium theme immediately. Take your time, expand you audience, and when you begin to feel the insufficiencies of the free theme, and when you have the investment to make, at exactly that point invest on a premium theme.

Content is the King

Content is the core of a blog and on the other hand that you need to be a fruitful blogger, your content must be superb. Content falls in one of the accompanying two classes: 1) Evergreen content or 2) High rise content.

Note: Blog content/articles/posts/points are various names for something very similar. Additionally, when I state 'traffic', I mean the quantity of guests to your blog.

Evergreen Content

As the name proposes, Evergreen content is made to be devoured until the end of time. The relativity of this eternity shifts, yet the fact is, the content is something which individuals frequently search independent of the present patterns.

For instance, in the event that I blog about music, at that point my blog post on the 'Historical backdrop of the Guitar' will qualify as Evergreen content in light of the fact that independent of what occurs in the music business, a few level of my group of spectators will consistently be intrigued to know the 'Historical backdrop of the Guitar'.

Evergreen content is more enthusiastically to make however. You need to look into, articulate focuses, and the vast majority of the occasions, the length of the post is longer than normal. It is a high reward game however, who wouldn't need a blog present that proceeds on get traffic independent of the patterns? You could just concentrate on making Evergreen content yet it would require a great deal of time and exertion. So how can one equalization it? By making Skyscraper content.

Skyscraper Content

As the name proposes, Skyscraper content has a mind blowing spike in enthusiasm for a short measure of time, which at that point goes down impressively — exhibiting an intrigue chart that looks like a Skyscraper.

So I'm not catching my meaning by intrigue? Indeed, I might want to give you a model: Apple Inc. is one of the most noticeable cell phone makers on the planet, and its iPhone offers to millions over the globe. Assume Apple Inc. reports it will dispatch its most recent iPhone one month from today. Presently the individuals who have innovation interests will scan for the news on the freshest iPhone. They need to know when it will dispatch, how much will it cost, and so forth.

These energetic individuals will play out a great deal of looks for the iPhone on a web search tool like Google.com. So web search tools will furnish them with sites that have content identifying with the most recent iPhone. Therefore, the greater part of the tech blogs with iPhone content will get various guests.

Enthusiasm for the iPhone will remain at its pinnacle even after its official dispatch, yet then it will take off down after about a month. That is the thing that Skyscraper content is, immense spike of enthusiasm for a short measure of time.

Skyscraper content is centered around current and drifting points. Composing it expects you to look into news and the most recent happenings in your favored specialty. For a photography blogger, it may be another Camera model or Lens, or Stilettos might incline for a Fashion blogger. It all relies upon the specialty.

Skyscraper Content is simpler to compose as there is a ton of important data accessible and the posts need not be the length of they are for Evergreen content. On the other hand, you may get captured up simply making Skyscraper content for the blog, which is certifiably not a decent arrangement when you are thinking long haul.

Presently you are thinking, would it be advisable for me to compose Evergreen or Skyscraper content for my blog? The key is not picking one sort of content and going bonkers with it yet making a blend of Evergreen just as Skyscraper content with a recurrence that you can continue. It is fundamental to have a brilliant harmony between the two sorts of content.

Evergreen content is more earnestly to make, so you could conceivably make one Evergreen content for each five bits of Skyscraper content. Along these lines, you find some kind of harmony. The abovementioned proportion is nonexclusive, for certain specialties, it might be considerably harder to make Evergreen content, and if that is the situation, you can attempt a 1:10 proportion for example one Evergreen content for each ten bits of Skyscraper content. Everything relies upon your specialty yet attempt to keep up equalization.

Here is my optimal system for content: If you are a blogging apprentice, I would encourage you not to distribute a great deal of Evergreen content immediately and center more around Skyscraper content. I explicitly utilize the word distribute. You can compose and stack your Evergreen content, however don't distribute every last bit of it a little while ago.

For what reason do I say this? When you are new to the blogging scene, treat your Evergreen content like gold. Give us a chance to state that you distribute an incredible Evergreen article, it is one of your generally outstanding work to date, however your blog is generally new, so regardless of whether individuals scan for the subject you have composed your article on, your article connection will rank lower than that of settled blogs. So why let it all out immediately? Demonstrate some of them now and hold the remaining ones for some other time. Your Evergreen content merits a more extensive crowd, have tolerance, and it will get what it merits.

Tips for creating Skyscraper Content

As you need more Skyscraper content, here are a few hints for making incredible Skyscraper content:

- **List it all**

Give us a chance to begin with a model, suppose you need to purchase a cell phone. Rather than looking the Web for cell phones and looking at them, you choose to locate a conclusive rundown of the best cell phones in your value run, so you look for 'Best Smartphones under $500'.

Your list items demonstrate various alternatives and you click on an article titled, 'Top 5 Cell phones under $500 for 2019'. Presently, the article has a distinct rundown of five alternatives limited down for your benefit. That is the thing that rundowns speak to, strong, exact arrangements of choices that offer a great deal of data and help the guest settle on a superior decision.

Records can be of anything; you could make a rundown of 'top 5 things not to', 'top 10 activities', 'top 5 interesting points', and so forth. The mental bit of leeway of records is that they give a feeling of validity to you as a blogger. At the point when an individual visits your rundown article, they realize that the rundown will contain a sifted, numbered request of components that won't beat around the hedge and convey exact data.

It is fundamental to abstain from posting such a large number of things. We as people will in general get confounded when somebody presents us with various alternatives. An article by the name 'Top 100 Books to understand this summer' sounds debilitating and is probably going to be skipped by a potential guest who would prefer perusing a 'Main 7 Books to peruse this midyear' article. Top3, top5, top 10 are the best sorts of rundown articles.

So go on at that point, check the news in your specialty and make 'list articles' that mirror the most recent patterns.

- **My 2 Cents Articles:**

Notwithstanding your specialty, there's something continually occurring in this enormous intense online world. As a blogger, you can compose or make content encompassing the most recent worldwide undertakings considering it your 2 Cents on it.

For instance, on the other hand that I am a photography blogger and there was an announcement from a superstar proposing, "Picture takers are exaggerated, the hardware tallies". I could then make a blog post titled, 'My 2 Cents on the big name's announcement'. 2 penny articles are incredible as they draw in a considerable amount of traffic in view of the slanting themes. Likewise, the post is depicted as your assessment of the subject, which is in every case superior to you being legitimately associated with the issue.

Along these lines, check the news in your specialty and see what themes you could drop your two cents on. Keep in mind however; you don't need to make the post disputable or cheeky only for it. Give your legitimate supposition regarding the matter with obligation.

Records and 2 penny articles are simpler to compose and are incredible for somebody who's simply getting begun as a blogger. Be that as it may, these are not by any means the only methods for making Skyscraper content. Look for the patterns in your specialty and concoct content that rotates around it.

Since you think about content, it's an ideal opportunity to keep in touch with some for the blog. It is perfect to dispatch the blog with in any event 4-5 articles/posts and afterward keep transferring content at a recurrence you can imaginatively coordinate. At the point when another guest sees that you have 4-5 posts transferred, it guarantees them that you are focused on giving content normally. In the prior section, I instructed you to make a harsh rundown of points for blog posts. Presently it's a great opportunity to utilize this rundown to make articles. As I've recommended in the past section, demonstrate your commitment by distributing at any rate 4-5 bits of content to begin with.

General tips for content

Regardless of whether you are composing Skyscraper or Evergreen content, the nature of your composing is of vital significance. An elegantly composed 400-word blog post will be cheered than an inadequately composed 800-word post.

Underscore on nature of your content as opposed to concentrating on the length of a blog post. Think about what worth you are including with your blog post. Here are a few hints for improving the nature of your content:

1. Intro – Main – Outro

The best essayists on the planet have a perfect method for getting you into a subject. They construct a story from an introduction that gets you energized for what's coming inside the fundamental part, and once they pass on their line of reasoning, they tenderly escort you to the entryways, leaving you with very much an experience.

Not we all are extraordinary book writers; however we can be incredible bloggers. We can utilize the equivalent system that each book writer does: Start with an introduction which is even more an inquiry to the pursuer, lead them to the appropriate response and let them ingest it, at that point close with an outro. As apparent as this method sounds, you will be astounded how frequently individuals neglect to tail it.

A lot of you may state, "Well, we get the procedure part however shouldn't something be said about the composition? We are not extraordinary scholars with flawless language structure and sentence structure." "We didn't peruse three books every week to build up a significant jargon"; trust me, I've inquired similar inquiries when I began blogging however here's something I wish I knew previously:

The best journalists on the planet are regularly respected so on the grounds that they are incredible storytellers and the best storytellers are frequently extraordinary at discussions. We all have in any event one individual in our life who is a delight to converse with, they tune in to what we need to state, assimilate it, remark on it and afterward set forth their two cents. We can converse with this individual for quite a long time on a stretch and never get exhausted. Thus, consider somebody like this in your life.

Things being what they are, could it be that makes you need to converse with this individual for a considerable length of time on a stretch? Is it their language structure that you venerate? Some of the time, you may appreciate their language structure, yet the vast majority of the occasions; it's their capacity to stream with a subject in an unconcerned manner. They simply realize when to tune in and when to talk. As a blogger, you have to try to be this Conversationalist. Syntax, sentence structure and everything else can be dealt with, yet the discussion part is basic.

2. Proof reading the Draft and making it Final:

A Draft is a work in advancement. When you have composed the blog post, we'll consider it a Draft as we are yet to alter it. We'll check this draft for punctuation, structure, and spelling blunders.

I won't request that you procure a supervisor yet rather download one!

'Grammarly' and 'Pro Writing Aid' are two of the most well-known online editor's accessible right presently. I utilize Grammarly Premium to alter my work, and the greater part of the occasions, it demonstrates enough yet you need not put resources into Grammarly Premium a little while ago.

The essential variant of Grammarly is completely free, and it's fantastic at discovering spelling botches, you can visit 'www.grammarly.com' and pursue a free record. When you do, duplicate what's more, glue your Draft in the Grammarly Editor. Presently the supervisor will call attention to spelling and other essential slip-ups which you can address in the editorial manager itself.

Hang on! The altering isn't yet done. Presently we need to change to 'ProWritingAid' for some time. ProWritingAid offers a 14-day free preliminary for their top notch rendition, and I profoundly propose you sign available. Initially, go to 'www.prowritingaid.com' and pursue a record (it's free). At that point either scans for the free preliminary choice or go to the supervisor and glue some irregular content. When done, click on any of the checks and you'll get a spring up saying PWA will just check the initial 500 words, in the event that you need more, demand a preliminary or go premium, at that point click on the 'demand a preliminary alternative', as demonstrated as follows:

At that point you'll be taken to a page where you have to enter your email address, like the one beneath:

After you enter your email address, you will get advised by email about the free preliminary endorsement. When you do, reorder your revised Draft (from Grammarly) into the PWA (ProWritingAid) manager and run the accompanying keeps an eye on it, as demonstrated as follows:

Note: Remember to uncheck the 'ongoing' alternative as it puts an excess of burden on the proofreader

The checks appeared above are the fundamental ones. You can go for more in the event that you need. When you fix the errors in PWA, it's a great opportunity to peruse the Draft for one final time before distributing. Peruse out boisterous and make revisions if fundamental. When you are done, you can distribute the post.

Grammarly and PWA are bits of programming, and as proficient as they may be, they aren't people, so now and again they need setting and report it as a blunder, this is the place you disregard the adjustment furthermore, go on.

Make sure to experience Grammarly, PWA, and after that read it yourself. The exact opposite thing you need is a guest seeing a minor composition botch which can be humiliating, so don't be lethargic here furthermore, experience this editing procedure.

3. Picture is right

It is regularly said that words usually can't do a picture justice, and much of the time, it is. For individuals to peruse your blog posts, they have to tap on it, and for them to tap on it, your blog posts need to be exceptional. All things considered, you could have the best content on the planet, yet for individuals to tap on it, the post needs to have an extraordinary header picture.

The picture needs to pass on the article quickly however ought to never be misleading. Individuals regularly observe the picture first and afterward read the title. Your header picture needs to induce the guest to peruse the title and open the blog post.

So where would you be able to get great, top notch pictures for your blog posts? All things considered, numerous sites offer brilliant pictures, yet they do charge a premium. No, we are not purchasing pictures yet. I told you previously, 'No additionally spending'. We are going 'With the expectation of complimentary Stock Images'. These are transferred by gifted picture takers to pick up introduction for their work. A portion of these pictures require Attribution, which includes referencing the Photographer/Up loader's name and subtleties in a few way or structure when you utilize their pictures.

Coming up next is where you can get these 'Free Stock Images':

- pexels.com
- www.freephotos.cc
- www.unsplash.com

- www.littlevisuals.co

- www.gratisography.com

Make sure to check the attribution status on the Image page.

Note: The Stock pictures that Photographers transfer on the above destinations require a ton of exertion to click and transfer. These Photographers are giving us something that they could some way or another be paid for, so regardless of whether attribution isn't required, give it in however conceivable. Online civility is uncommon, yet that doesn't mean you shouldn't tail it.

4. A word on content frequency

It is basic to choose the content recurrence of your blog. Ask yourself, what number of articles will I innovatively finish in seven days? The significance here lies in imaginatively. Hurrying through composing seven articles in seven days isn't right; it denies you of your innovativeness and trustworthiness. It is alright to compose 1-2 articles every week, as long as you can give it equity.

As your blog develops well known, it is vital that you keep up a degree of consistency with your content. You can't be posting eight articles in a single week and none in the following week. You can stack great bits of content on the other hand that you like and post them once all is good and well.

Consistency consistently triumphs with regards to content. A blogger who just posts once per week yet, does it for a long time is unquestionably bound to be pursued than somebody who goes off the framework subsequent to posting 20 articles in about fourteen days. Take a gander at your every day and week by week calendars and plan your content recurrence. Keep in mind, quality and not amount matters.

How to make Money from the Blog

Ideally, individuals won't pursue cash. They would be satisfied with whatever they have and go on with their lives. Be that as it may, it isn't so. Cash has picked up this fundamental significance throughout everyday life; in addition to the fact that it is vital for our extravagances our day by day needs. So I could continue forever about how everybody should simply cherish what they do and life will be loaded up with rainbows and unicorns yet then I would lie. You have to acquire cash from your blog, and you will, however ensure it isn't the main explanation you blog. Here's the reason I am so against on lucrative destinations: Suppose your solitary objective is to make $500 this month, presently regardless of whether you are working in the field you adore, defining an objective that rotates around a number tops your potential and the real cash you can make.

Give me a chance to expound with a model: Suppose I am a photography blogger, and I have increased a following of 10,000 individuals on my blog. Presently if my lone objective is to by one way or another make $500 this month, at that point this objective of mine will make me need to take alternate routes any place fundamental, what not I can consider is the means by which I can utilize these 10,000 individuals to make me $500. So I may prescribe a camera I haven't looked into inside and out and post it on the blog saying it is the 'Best Camera Ever', to make sure I can pick up offshoot commission from it.

Presently the supporters of my blog trust my decision so much that some of them will wind up purchasing the camera since I am prescribing it. Also, when these individuals discover the camera isn't extraordinary all things considered, they won't confide in my decision any longer, and soon they will tell different supporters of my duplicity. The outcome is me nearly losing all that I've buckled down for, all since I needed to profit snappier.

Regardless of whether I made $500 that month, I denied myself of my devotees' trust and the potential cash that I could have made, had I been straightforward. Additionally, had I been straightforward, these 10,000 individuals would have prescribed the blog to various others, and my legitimate suggestions would have made me enough cash some place down the line.

For what reason did I shoot myself in the leg? Since I was pursuing cash, and I needed it speedy. Presently, I will disclose to you various approaches to profit from your blog. In the event that you pursue just cash however, no measure of intelligence will prevent you from fizzling.

Comprehend the strategies I let you know, practice their execution, and you will profit from your blog. Persistence is the key here, take a gander at it along these lines, would you need to make $200 this month immediately or make $100 every month for the following 6-7 months and arrive at a point where you can procure $500 per month. Have the persistence to see the master plan.

The rundown isn't in any request, and a few techniques are simpler for certain specialties than others and vice versa, so read and get them, and through execution, you'll realize what works for your specialty and what doesn't.

Affiliate Marketing

This strategy is the best method for profiting from your blog when you are simply firing up. Think about an affiliate as this center man that elevates items to individuals, and if individuals purchase those items through the affiliate's reference, the affiliate gets a commission from it.

Numerous individuals think Affiliate Marketing is sales rep marketing, which isn't valid in any way. A sales rep attempts to sell you items, their lone activity is to induce you to purchase their item, and as much as I value their abilities, you don't need to do that as an affiliate.

At whatever point you need to purchase an item on the pricier side, how would you choose on the other hand that you will get it or on the other hand not?

Indeed, first, you check the audits that different purchasers have left. For what reason do you do that? Indeed, you don't confide in the marketing contrivances that makers attempt to force, and you search for an assessment. Indeed, its visually impaired trust, yet it is more ameliorating than perusing arranged lines of advancement. We look for human counsel, and it sits as the fundamental factor in our purchasing choices. How often have you approached your loved ones for purchasing exhortation? A great deal I am speculating, since we confide in their assessment.

The perfect method to utilize Affiliate Marketing is to give genuine audits of the items in your specialty and afterward give your group of spectators a simpler decision to purchase the said items through an affiliate connect. First however, you should win your group of spectators' trust and mind you, it is the hardest to gain.

So how would you gain this trust? You should consistently give a fair-minded feeling on an item, news, or hypotheses. When you continue making such content, your group of spectators confides in you and considers you to be to some degree an Authoritative figure in your specialty.

Your specialty has items, regardless of whether Physical or Digital, and these items are sold at commercial centers. You as a blogger need to approach these commercial centers and search for their affiliate programs. In the event that you don't discover a connection on the landing page, keep in touch with them an email, and you will get an answer. There aren't numerous prerequisites for an affiliate program, yet it likewise relies upon your specialty.

On the other hand that the commercial center rejects your application saying you need more traffic on your blog, search for other confided in commercial centers and apply there. In the event that no commercial center acknowledges you at this minute, don't stress. Concentrate on improving your content, and you will arrive at the traffic necessities for the said affiliate programs.

When you are acknowledged to an affiliate program, you are presently qualified to make a commission. Nonetheless, you can't simply duplicate an Amazon connection and glue it on your blog and hope to make a Commission from it. Affiliate connections vary from ordinary connections, and as an affiliate, you gain admittance to an interface where you can make these affiliate joins, which you can glue on your blog.

One significant thing to recall is that the commercial center you are an affiliate of should be dependable. They may offer the best limits, yet do they convey on schedule? How would they handle item returns? Is their client assistance adequate? You have to look into in light of the fact that you are underwriting them to your supporters.

In the event that one of your devotees were to have a disagreeable encounter, they would feel let down, and you will be a piece of the fault. No commercial center is flawless. I've seen a lot of bungles from somebody as large as Amazon, yet the likelihood is less, so I more often than not suggest items from Amazon.

Do your exploration and rundown great, reliable destinations, and after that apply for their affiliate programs. In the event that you don't get in, don't take a stab at sub-par locales. Pause! You can generally concentrate on expanding your traffic. It is unmistakably progressively valuable to pause, increment your traffic and attempt again than making due with an average commercial center.

So you've gotten into a dependable commercial center, what next? All things considered, search for items in your specialty that you can audit. They don't need to be new. Take a gander at your storage room, see what you can find and audit it on the blog.

On the other hand that innovation and contraptions are my specialties and suppose I have a two-year-old Bluetooth speaker, I will make an audit on it and call it, 'How my JBL cut 1 endured me through 2 years of utilization'. Imagination is the name of the game. You need not purchase extravagant new items and audit them, acquire something from your companion, associate or family, use it for two days and compose an audit on it.

Affiliate Marketing will test your respectability however, suggesting a decent $300 cell phone which gives you less commission is superior to suggesting an unremarkable $1000 cell phone which gets you twofold the commission. Keep in mind, backing and survey items as though you are doing it for your friends and family in light of the fact that there isn't a lack of individuals needing that brisk buck, furthermore, I genuinely don't need you to be a piece of that circle. The Internet is an open book, so the majority of the individuals think about Affiliate Marketing, and I'd suggest you express a note toward the finish of your articles that state something like this:

"The above connection is an Affiliate connection and obtaining through the connection gives me a percent of the benefit which encourages me keep up this blog. I'd truly value it in the event that you made your buy through the above connection. Much appreciated.

The above message is authentic and warm. Your guests will welcome the straightforwardness and will eagerly utilize your connections at whatever point essential. Commercial centers have characterized commission rates for items, tech items have a littler commission yet cost more while garments offer higher commissions yet are less expensive. Commercial centers like Amazon and so forth showcase certain items more, when they do, they dispense the affiliate cash to marketing, thus on the other hand that you sell an item like that, you don't get a commission for it.

This doesn't mean you quit prescribing an extraordinary item. According to the Amazon Affiliate Model, when a client taps on your affiliate connection and arrives at a commercial center, a session starts, whatever the client at that point purchases in the session is enlisted as your deal, and you get the commission for it.

CPC, CPM and CPA Ad Network

Ever observe those Ads on the page you are perusing? These are called situation Ads, furthermore, the odds are, and you have seen them as of late. Additionally, these arrangement Ads by one way or another as it were show Ads significant to your perusing history, and no it is anything but a fortuitous event, yet that is a story for another page (see what I did there!).

Here is a case of situation Ads (checked red) on a blog:

Situation Ads can enable you to procure cash, however your blog needs extensive guest traffic for them to work. In any case, I should enlighten you concerning them, for when your blog arrives at huge guest traffic; you should execute them.

Some of you might need to actualize these immediately however you shouldn't and here's an model why: There is this vehicle magazine that has recently been discharged, and as an early on offer, it is accessible for least cost. Inquisitive about what's inside, individuals get it and to their shock, the content is amazing, the magazine here has not many ads in the middle of which makes the experience more flow than different magazines in a similar specialty.

Having not very many Ads gives the pursuer a smoother experience, and they don't feel like the magazine is simply forcing Ads on them. This grows better trust with the pursuers of the magazine, and thus, the magazine gets various enrollments.

Thus, when your blog is new, you need minimal measure of interruptions, which makes for a better guest experience which will give you additionally returning traffic. So for the present, center around traffic, furthermore, when you increase a respectable after, at that point read the beneath segment once more:

To begin with, let me reveal to you why these arrangement Ads appear to be so pertinent to your perusing history:

When you visit a commercial center like Amazon or perform look on locales like Google, these sites keep up a little document about it called a 'Treat' which has little data on what you've scanned for. So whenever you visit a site that has situation ads, these ads are given the Cookie which makes them show Ads important to your hunts. Presently, this may feel like an interruption of security, and somewhat it is, yet that is the expense of utilizing administrations from these organizations.

On the other hand that you need to run position Ads on your blog, you have to approach an Ad Network. These are administrations which help interface the blogger with the promoters, and they do take a portion of the benefit, yet with all that they accomplish for us, it is a little cost to pay. So before you approach an Ad Network, you should think about 'Income Models'.

Income models were created as a standard for bloggers, sponsors and Ad Networks the same, so you should think about them. Here are some prevalent income models:

CPC (Cost per Click) Revenue Model

In this income model you are paid as per the quantity of clicks enlisted on a specific advertisement. As I've said previously, these are directed advertisements, so the odds of somebody tapping on it are higher than expected. Keep in mind, you are paid per click, regardless of whether the guest winds up purchasing the item/administration or not. As a blogging beginner, this model is incredible for you, as you needn't bother with tremendous measures of traffic to get clicks. The Ad-systems characterize a Cost for every Click rate, which could be anything between $0.50 furthermore, $3.

Cost per Mille (CPM) Revenue Model

The CPM model pays the blogger as indicated by the quantity of guest Impressions on a specific Ad. These are typically estimated on a for each thousand impressions premise. At the point when a guest drifts their mouse over the Ad, without clicking it, it is enrolled as an impression.

The CPM rate is fixed by the Ad-arrange and can be anything somewhere in the range of $2 and $5 per

1000 impressions. This model works incredible with progressively huge traffic, so when you arrive at a greater group of spectators, this model will suit you better.

Cost Per Action (CPA) Model

As the name proposes, the CPA model works just when a client clicks on a promotion and finishes an activity. The promoter characterizes the activity, which can be anything from filling a couple of subtleties to finishing a buy. The CPA rate at that point relies upon what activity the publicist requires, the more drawn out the activity the better the CPA rate. CPA model pays a great deal of cash for an effective activity. Be that as it may, the likelihood of guests tapping on a promotion and finishing further activity is low. To prevail at this model, your blog needs a huge amount of traffic as the likelihood of the finish is low.

The above were the diverse income models, and now I'll show some well-known Ad Networks that you can approach. You don't need to do a lot, simply pursue a record first, and enter the subtleties of your blog and you are a great idea to go:

Keep in mind, you don't need to pick just a single income model, you can join to three distinctive Ad Networks and send all the three income models together. Be that as it may, as another blogger, you would squander a great deal of Ad Space in the event that you execute CPM and CPA Ads immediately, so my advice is start with conveying CPC ads, and as your traffic develops, you can explore different avenues regarding CPM and CPA Ads. It's critical to analyze however, when your traffic develops then you change between diverse Ad-networks and Revenue models and see what works best for you.

Renting Ad Space

You can sell Advertising Space on your blog to individuals ready to advertise. This technique gives you the opportunity to charge as you wish and gives you unlimited oversight. In any case, to execute this strategy, your blog must have extensive traffic, and you have to demonstrate these insights to advertisers ready to partake.

This strategy isn't productive enough for another blogger. When you have an impressive sum of traffic that is the point at which you can make the most out of this technique. You can compose a message like the one underneath to tell your crowd that you are willing to lease Ad Space:

Need 10,000 month to month guests to see your Product or Service?

We are leasing Advertising Space on our blog, on the other hand that you are intrigued, Contact Us Now.

The advantages of this technique are enormous, you get the opportunity to keep all the cash, you choose the expense, and what's more, you have full power over it.

Above were some simpler and moral methods for profiting from your blog yet these techniques will be powerful just when you make significant substance. Also, the best way to make incredible substance is to concentrate on it and not on the cash.

Why isn't a traditional Blog enough?

So for what reason isn't a blog on a website enough? All things considered, it was sufficient around ten years prior, however now things have changed, and they generally will. Each time you give individuals the opportunity to express themselves; they will discover new and inventive approaches to contact a greater group of spectators, which results in increasingly content.

Presently I have to lease/purchase a spot for my store, so I scan for the equivalent and I locate the ideal place for me. It's luxurious enough for my need and sits on one of the most well-known avenues in town. Be that as it may, is an extraordinary area enough for me to get clients? No, I have to make individuals mindful of the shop and for that; I have to advertise. Regardless of whether I am the best cook on the planet, potential clients will possibly think about the pastry kitchen when I advance it. So how would I advertise it?

I could print a paper Ad, all things considered; it is perhaps the most seasoned mode of data that individuals read day by day. Alright, so I post an advertisement on the most powerful paper around the local area trusting individuals will read it and walk around for a visit.

Have I done all the better I could do?

Consider it. Suppose the town has a populace of 50,000. Of these, what number of do you think read the paper day by day? I will say 30-35%, in light of the fact that cutting edge times have presented new vehicles of data, and individuals aren't that slanted to read papers any longer. So how do I advertise to the remainder of the populace?

Turns out the town has a famous nearby radio channel, so to elevate the pastry kitchen to the dynamic radio audience members around the local area, I put an advert on the radio channel. Be that as it may, shouldn't something be said about young people matured 15-19 or adults matured 20-30? The vast majority of them neither read the paper nor do they tune in to the radio. The most ideal approach to contact this group of spectators is to be available in a medium where they are: Social Media. In the event that I need to contact a bigger group of spectators, I have to advance my business via web-based networking media.

I am utilizing these consideration channels to manufacture a brand for my bread shop. Regardless of whether the business doesn't get guests immediately, I need to spread mindfulness among the majority of its reality. I've contacted my group of spectators dependent on their inclination of medium, some read papers, the composed word medium. Some tune in to the radio, a perceptible medium while some expended web based life, a blended medium.

I can't anticipate that radio audience members should leave their favored stage and all of a sudden start reading papers, that'd be silly. I have to arrive at their preferred medium, and not the other way around.

Every medium has its quirks. A paper ad ought not to be a 500-word article. It ought to be exact on the grounds that individuals don't have the opportunity to read a 500-word advertisement. On the other hand, radio Ads should be speedy, snappy and straightforward on the grounds that individuals would prefer not to tune in to an Ad which endures more than 15 seconds, so the test is to hold it under 15 seconds yet still pass on the message. Web based life has its quirks also. Facebook is appropriate for longer posts while Twitter isn't, YouTube is all video while webcasts aren't. The Ads must be custom fitted for what works best on a stage.

Like the model above, blogging is currently broader than at any other time. To arrive at bigger spectators, your blog must be available where they are, instead of them leaving their liked stage to go to yours.

Tailor your content dependent on a stage to increase most extreme outcomes. The objective here is to increment your image esteem, so individuals partner you as a specialty master, and when they do, it brings you various chances to profit while doing what you adore. Your blog is never again composed word, its content in all shapes and structures. I'll enable you to spread your blog to all media imaginable, yet we'll begin delayed by setting up our blog channels via web-based networking media.

Socialize with Social Media

As a consumer, I am not a major fanatic of online life, I trust it makes a bigger number of issues than it unravels. Nonetheless, as a content maker, I couldn't be more infatuated with it. We as makers should be available where the consumers are, and not a different way. Internet based life is an outright aid for content makers around the globe, and whenever utilized right, it can offer you with ten times consideration.

Before we grow the blog, you should build up your essence on prominent social media stages viz. Facebook, Twitter and Instagram. There are various different stages you may need, yet for the present; we should concentrate on these three.

Initially, you should make pages on Facebook and Instagram for your blog. On Twitter, you should make another record. Also, these pages/accounts need to have a similar name as your blog.

When done, we have to build up a ceaseless visual intrigue over all stages. For this, we'll need a Logo. Presently, except if you are a Graphics Designer, I will profoundly propose you get a Logo made for the blog. It won't cost a lot, and you can discover independent designers on locales, for example, Fiverr, who'd do it for five dollars. You have a state in how the logo should look, so simply ensure the logo isn't excessively occupied. Most

Learner bloggers attempt to pack all of their blog into the logo, which isn't the best approach. Effortlessness consistently triumphs in any type of plan, and that is the reason the best designers regularly make the least difficult of plans.

Likewise, you should tell your Graphics Designer that you'll be utilizing the logo on practically all the social media stages. Along these lines, you'll need various renditions of the logo explicit to different locales.

A decent logo goes far; it enables the blog to look more genuine, and that is the reason you have to get it planned by an expert. Regardless of whether you aren't planning the logo, there's something I call the 'Brilliant Rule of Design' which you should know: No Form over Function. This implies no structure of visual upgrade should influence the utilitarian piece of the plan.

A logo is little, so you don't have a lot of space to work with. Simply recall, your logo structure must pass on the blog on the principal look. Here is a case of a spotless logo plan:

When the logo is dealt with, set the spread photograph with indistinguishable hues from your logo. Or then again you can upload a picture that matches your blog specialty. The spread photograph is the picture that lies in the foundation of a showcase picture. The spread photograph for the above logo should look something like this:

Ensure each of the three stages have a similar logo and spread photograph. Presently you have an essential structure congruity over the stages. I'll instruct you with these social media accounts, on the whole, we should be on YouTube.

Expansion YouTube

Here are a couple details on YouTube discharged by YouTube during one of its public statements in 2019: Makers upload more than 500 hours of video on it consistently, and in excess of 250 million hours of content are viewed on TV screens each and every day.

So if individuals are viewing a gazillion recordings consistently, for what reason wouldn't one be able to of them be yours? Why botch the chance to expand your crowd? I've referenced this previously: you can't anticipate individuals to leave their favored stages to join yours, you must be available on their favored stage.

Give me a chance to explain a significant confusion that individuals have with respect to making recordings on YouTube: It's about what you state and not what you look like. It makes me insane what number of individuals keeps themselves away from YouTube on the grounds that they think they are not entirely enough to be on camera.

I used to feel a similar way. Also, I think it originated from watching films and VIPs when I was growing up. How precisely? All things considered, viewing these big names with their radiant skin, conditioned muscles and natural capacity to battle outsiders and changing robots constantly made me wonder, what it must resemble to act in a motion picture. It additionally intentionally or something else, made me feel that on the other hand that I need to be before the camera, I should resemble a Superstar. I realize I am not alone who felt thusly, and I do trust it is the explanation a lot of individuals are as yet hesitant to record a video of themselves for YouTube.

So let me clear it for you: When individuals watch a YouTube video, they aren't searching for beautiful faces. They are searching for worth. It isn't about what you look like, however what you need to state. In the event that you can offer some benefit to your group of spectators, at that point it doesn't make a difference what you look like or what things you have out of sight. I can actually make a video in my lounge room disclosing how to make cash web based wearing the most essential garments, chaotic hair, and a heap of filthy garments behind me, furthermore, it will even now get a huge amount of perspectives.

So don't feel unreliable about getting before the camera, don't think what your companions and family may think subsequent to viewing your recordings. You are here to make content for your group of spectators. Other individuals' assessment of you is not your issue to worry about.

Ideally I have washed down camera uneasiness from your side, if there was any. YouTube gives a huge open door for you to pick up introduction, don't miss it!

Make a YouTube account on the other hand that you don't have one, and set up the profile as you would on other social media stages, for example, uploading the blog logo as the presentation picture, changing the record name to the name of your blog, changing the spread picture, and so on. I won't discuss making recordings seconds ago. For the time being, it is about the arrangement. I'll talk about the video creation part later.

Expansion: Podcasting

Podcasting is the most blazing go-to stage for bloggers around the world. Everybody is going to digital recordings and there are a bunch of purposes behind it above all, we should characterize web recordings. A digital recording is like your very own radio show however instead of a radio set, it's accessible on the Internet through digital recording administrations. Web recordings are voice just as radio shows may be, yet they need almost no hardware to get begun. You can truly record digital broadcasts from your cell phone and upload them on the web.

Podcasting has turned out to be prevalent in the course of the most recent years due to its aloofness. When you watch a YouTube video, you are taking a gander at it and tuning in to it simultaneously. With web recordings however, you can hear them out while accomplishing different things, which empowers you to perform various tasks.

As a blogger in 2019, you should have a webcast appear for your blog. There are a huge number of individuals tuning in to web recordings each and every day, so why waste the chance?

I will prescribe you to tune in to a couple webcast appears in a specialty of your advantage, particularly if you haven't heard a digital broadcast previously. Download a digital broadcast gushing application, for example, Spotify, Apple Music, or Google Podcasts and quest for digital broadcasts in your favored specialty. Digital broadcasts are an gained taste, so don't hope to be overwhelmed by them immediately.

To begin with, I'll talk about setting up a digital broadcast show, and after that we'll plunge into the content. After you are finished with the arrangement, I'll advise you to not pursue with the chronicle part, instead, read the next part about making content in a significantly more effective way.

The Setup

Like a website, you need a digital broadcast have for podcasting. A Podcast host will have your documents and give you an exceptional connection which you can use to stream your digital broadcast to Apps such as Spotify, Apple Music, Google Podcasts, and some more.

Indeed, you have to pay the podcast have for its administrations. When I began podcasting, I explored famous has and picked Podbean.com. One of the principle highlights it offers is, you get a free preliminary arrangement where you can upload four hours of podcast scenes every month. So you upload eight scenes of 30 minutes each, your portion for that month will end.

I utilized the preliminary for a month, got to know the eccentricities, and decided on a $10 month to month plan. Thus, for the present, you can pursue the free program; try out the waters and after that bounce further when you are ready.

The following is the methodology to set up a record on a podcast host, for example, Podbean. The strategies I notice are for Podbean.com however these are commonly the equivalent for different hosts.

1. Go to podbean.com and click on 'attempt podbean for nothing'.

2. Enter the subtleties and in the subdomain field, enter the name of your podcast. The title ought to incorporate your blog name. E.g., my blog 'tennis

fanatic' has a podcast called 'The Tennis Fnatic Podcast'. On the other hand that you would prefer not to appoint it at the present time, you can generally do it later.

3. Check your record by tapping on the connection sent to your email address. When the record is checked, fill in the subtleties, finish a name for the podcast, upload the blog logo (ideally you have made one) and now you are ready to go.

Recording a Podcast

Podcasts are lengthier than your normal YouTube video, and the length for the most part relies upon your specialty. A few specialties have scenes that are two hours drawn-out period of time some have 15 moment long scenes.

Go to a podcast gushing application/site like Spotify or iTunes, scan for podcasts in your specialty, check their normal run times and check whether you can create a podcast inside that run time. Podcasts don't need to be exact; you don't have to read word-by-word from content. Podcasts should have an easygoing, conversational tone to it and that is one of the fundamental reasons individuals tune in to podcasts.

Accepting you have made sense of the normal podcast scene time in your specialty, it's an ideal opportunity to record your absolute initially podcast scene. A podcast scene can be a gathering of various sections or a solitary broad portion, contingent upon the subject obviously.

Note: Now I'll be clarifying how you can record your first podcast scene. Be that as it may, you need not adhere to the guidelines immediately. I'll be disclosing how to make content more proficiently in the following section.

For your first scene, look at the news in your specialty, waitlist the ones that energize you, and record your assessments of the equivalent. Despite the fact that you needn't bother with content, it's a decent practice to compose the briefest review of the scene. Along these lines, you recall what you need to state, and at that point you can grow it in your own words.

For instance, in the event that my podcast rotates around technology and gadgets, at that point my first scene review will look something like this:

Episode 1:

Portion 1: Apple iPhone X battery issues, the truth and my assessment of it.

Fragment 2: My contemplations on the forthcoming Google Pixel 3.

Fragment 3: Discussing my preferred Android round ever.

The outline is for you, not for your crowd. When you are recording, you frequently overlook the directs you need toward make, so the outline causes you to keep up a stream. As should be obvious in the above model, the diagram is brief so I can develop it in my very own words. What's more, that is the reason you needn't bother with content, however you do require a short diagram, so think of one for your scene.

Podcasts are sound just, which means you just have one medium to enrapture the group of spectators. In this way, sound quality is significant here. You should sound clear to the group of spectators; generally, the close catch is rarely far away. Set up podcasters utilize top notch receivers to record their podcasts, yet you need not make any venture of that sort at the present time.

I recorded my podcast scenes on my smartphone for the initial three months, at that point when I had enough cash to contribute; I put resources into a $60 Podcast Mic.

Each smartphone has a sound notice/recorder application as a matter of course, and we will require this application to record our podcast scenes. In the event that your smartphone doesn't have one, download one from the application store immediately. Presently you have to locate a calm spot to record, wherever is fine as long as it is peaceful. Presently keep the composed scene diagram before you and start recording.

Here are few recording tips:

1. Smartphone amplifiers are omnidirectional, so regardless of whether there is clamor toward the path inverse to you, despite everything it'll lift it up, so ensure the space that you are recording in is commotion free.

2. Podcasts are easygoing, so be normal; there is no compelling reason to sound automated by reading from a content. The 'umms' and the 'ahhs' are satisfactory, even little stops are. Accept you are talking to a dear companion; simply keep a tab on the condemnations however!

3. Try not to attempt to record the ideal scene since it doesn't exist. You can just record an incredible scene when you are having a great time doing it, so unwind and simply let it stream. Keep in mind that we have an altering procedure after this, where we can address nearly everything.

When you have recorded the scene, it's an ideal opportunity to alter. Give me a chance to reveal to you something: There isn't a podcaster throughout the entire existence of the world who has distributed a decent podcast scene without altering, so realize that you have to do it. For altering, it is smarter to utilize a Desktop PC or a Laptop, in the event that you don't have one, download a sound proofreader application on your smartphone/tablet.

Presently the great people of the Internet have furnished us with an outright diamond of an altering device in 'Boldness'. It is allowed to download, and you can download it here:

Presently move your recorded sound document to the PC and open it in Audacity. There are a plenty of simple instructional exercises for Audacity altering on YouTube, attempt and watch them. When you alter the document, spare it. Presently we have to upload our first ever podcast scene.

The uploading part is clear, go to your podcast have dashboard, and snap on 'upload scene' (or a comparable choice). At that point to the altered sound record, fill in the subtleties of the scene and you are finished.

Presently the podcast is live, and you get a 'xml feed' in the dashboard, this is the connection I was discussing prior. Podcast gushing destinations need this connection, when they have it, they separate the insights regarding the podcast from it. You have to post this connection (xml feed) alongside data on your podcast to gushing applications/destinations. Go to locales like Apple Music, Spotify, and Google Podcasts to present your podcast.

When you present your podcast, each time you make a scene, you just need to upload it on your host, at that point as you have connected the 'xml feed' to the gushing administrations, they separate everything including the most up to date scenes as you upload them. So you need not upload each podcast scene to each spilling site/application.

Like I've referenced previously, I'd help you set up every one of these stages first and after that give you the methodology to make content. Ideally, you've set up the stages, on the other hand that you haven't, kindly don't continue.

The Pillar Content Strategy

The Content Problem

I guided you to be available on all the social media stages and make custom-made substance as indicated by the qualities of the stage however it is a troublesome undertaking to draw off. Composing content for explicit stages, over and over, can, and will deplete you. So how can one be present on every one of the stages, make content consistently, and still have sanity?

The Pillar Content Strategy

Content is one; mediums are extraordinary. A touring blog present on a get-away on Bali is one bit of content. In any case, on the other hand that you need to disperse it over every one of the stages, you'll have to make various renditions of it, and those injuries up to be a serious undertaking!

So how can one arrangement with this circumstance? You can't extend your arrive at except if your blog is present on all the important stages, however making various adaptations of a similar content will take heaps of time. I experienced a similar issue, until I unearthed a content methodology made by Gary Vaynerchuk, a showcasing master and business person, called the 'Gary Vee Content Model Deck'. He has magnanimously made the technique open to open, so on the other hand that you need to understand more, scan on the Internet for the equivalent. Gotten from Gary Vaynerchuk's Model Deck, I have made a content methodology explicit for blogging. I like to call it 'The Pillar Content' technique. So what's going on here? How would you execute it?

The strategy includes making Pillar content with the end goal that you can separate it into various mediums according to a stage. Let's assume you record a video of yourself assessing a football coordinate among Barcelona and Real Madrid (furious competition among football clubs). By chronicle a video, you've made Pillar content, which has the potential for three mediums: video, sound and content. When you alter the video, you can transfer it on video spilling locales, for example, YouTube, Facebook video, IGTV and so forth., at that point you can separate the sound from the video and transfer it as a web recording scene and when you decipher the video, you can distribute it as an article/post speaking to the composed word medium.

Generally, you'd record a video, alter it, and after that transfer on video gushing destinations. At that point, you'd record its sound rendition, alter it, and after that transfer it. Lastly you'd compose a composed word adaptation, alter it and after that transfer it as an article/post. The 'Pillar Content' strategy does likewise assignments thrice as quick, so why burn through your time following the customary content strategy?

The most ideal method for making Pillar content is to record a video. At the point when you do as such, you get a video, a separate sound, and a no frills content. YouTube, Facebook and IGTV have a level of group of spectators that will watch the whole video regardless of whether it is long, these are where you can transfer the Pillar recordings for what it's worth.

At the point when you separate the sound from these Pillar recordings you get the 'Pillar Audio' which at that point with a little introduction and outro can be transferred as a webcast scene. I've referenced previously, webcast group of spectators likes to tune in to long term sound, so except if your Pillar video was ludicrously enormous for your specialty, you can transfer your 'Pillar Audio' as a digital recording scene.

You additionally have a stripped down content, you can either grow that content, clean it and make a site blog post or add an introduction to it and transfer it for what it's worth. At the point when you do this, you presently have with yourself 'Pillar composed word' content which you can transfer all things considered on the site and at that point alter it to make sub-material for answers, remarks, and so forth.

Now, we have three mechanisms of Pillar content accessible however we'll be squandering a great deal of potential for our content on the other hand that we don't change over it into Micro and Macro. So let the altering start.

To begin with, we'll center around the Macro, at that point we go to the Micro.

Full scale content is altered from the pillar content so that it offers some benefit without anyone else without a requirement for any more pillar content. For instance, If your pillar content is 'Bali Travel Video blog' at that point you can alter your pillar content and make full scale content, for example, 'how to go to Bali from Europe', 'how to discover less expensive lodgings in Bali' or '5 spots to find in Bali'. Keep in mind; you don't need to shoot new content for the full scale. All you have to will be to alter your pillar content with the goal that it can remain without anyone else.

Instagram licenses a 1-minute video (not IGTV). YouTube, Facebook Video, IGTV, Twitter have a group of people for Smaller recordings too, these are where you can transfer 'Full scale' video content from the 'Pillar Video' content. On the other hand that your 'Pillar Video' can't be partitioned into 1- minute recordings, at that point don't concentrate on Instagram recordings for the time being, we can generally get it in the Small scale. See what your group of spectators might need to watch in a nutshell, include an appropriate introduction and outro if fundamental, and afterward transfer these recordings.

Twitter used to just permit 30-second recordings, yet it has now stretched out it to 140 seconds, so you can transfer recordings as long as 2 minutes 20 seconds in length. On the other hand that you can tailor your video content to that farthest point, at that point pull out all the stops. If not, you can generally share your 'Miniaturized scale' recordings with a proper sub-content. Something like, "In the event that you need to figure out how to get the best low-light pictures on your cell phone, at that point watch the fundamental video", and connection the video.

On the other hand that you're 'Pillar Audio' is unreasonably huge for a web recording, you can generally alter it in parts and make sub scenes, include an introduction and an outro and cause numerous to digital recording scenes with these sub scenes. In the event that not, at that point leave it, we'll generally have a chance to utilize the 'Pillar Audio' later.

The 'Pillar composed word' has a great deal of potential for the 'Macro'. Start with Quora answers, find appropriate inquiries, include a composed introduction and outro, and glue reasonable pieces of the Pillar content. You can do this for a few answers yet ensure your alters are applicable and don't beat as well much around the hedge. You can end your answers with something like, "This concentrate is a piece of the first post on my blog (site), click here to see the full post".

The other method to make 'macro' from 'Pillar composed word' is to make sub-articles from it. Presently, this may not make a difference all over the place, yet when you have the chance, you can execute this system. The sub-articles will be perused by individuals who would prefer not to peruse the whole post what's more, are keen on particulars. For E.g., a Travel Blog present on your visit on Spain is the 'Pillar composed content', which can be separated into sub-posts like, '5 activities before you visit Spain', '5 spots you should visit in Spain', 'How I went on a dainty Budget to Spain', '5 well known dishes to eat when you're in Spain' and so forth.

With the expansion of posting these sub-articles on the blog, you can likewise distribute them on sites like Medium, where individuals get a chance to compose articles on their preferred points furthermore, get presentation to a huge group of spectators. When you contact a greater group of spectators, Medium even gets you paid. Contingent upon your 'Pillar composed word' content, you can get great presentation on Medium. Medium just supports installment in select nations for the time being, however soon they'll be extending to different nations.

As should be obvious in the above model, I made various sub-articles from a Pillar article. The key is to comprehend what your crowd may jump at the chance to peruse in a nutshell and following up on it. This won't come simple, obviously! Give it time and you'll realize your group of spectators better.

Presently we have our Pillar content earning consideration all alone, at that point we have 'Macro' content helping it in transit, and now it's the ideal opportunity for 'Miniaturized scale' content. Entryways, for example, Twitter, Instagram are incredible for Micro, yet you have to tailor the content to exploit these stages. Twitter just permits 160 words, you can outline your Macro or Pillar content and connection to these. For instance, you can share your Pillar Video of the Bali trip as: I made a trip to Bali in under $1000. To realize what I checked, out the principle video.

You can do likewise for composed content, abridge the content and after that connect to the primary blog post as 'Here is the manner by which I spent just $1000 on my Bali trip'. The key is to outline Macro or Pillar content and guide the group of spectators to it.

Instagram permits photographs, 1-minute recordings and a 30-second story. On the other hand that you can alter your Pillar Video or Macro Video content into a 1-minute video, at that point do it. In the event that you can't, alter out a bit that condenses a point, and after that direct the crowd to the IGTV connect in the event that they need to see the full video. Same applies to Instagram stories.

You can post related photographs and connection to IGTV also. For instance, on the other hand that I have Pillar Macro content on profiting from podcasting, I'd post a photograph of my podcasting rigging saying something like, 'Here is my Podcasting Gear. I as of late did a video on the most proficient method to profit from Podcasting, here's the video'.

Facebook and YouTube both take into account stories now, so you can apply your Instagram stories content here. Despite the fact that YouTube and Facebook stories are new, they will make up for lost time, so why not start now?

At the point when you are done, you have three degrees of content in every one of the mediums, took into account the group of spectators as indicated by their needs. Each piece of this accumulation remains solitary without anyone else while giving introduction to different parts. All aspects of content is bringing you consideration, and in the procedure, it is expanding your image esteem. The more presentation you get, the more group of spectators will know you and will begin to confide in you. The majority of this introduction opens numerous entryways of openings.

The Pillar Content strategy is extraordinary for productivity yet can overpower you before all else. So start moderate, you don't have to deliver Macro and Micro content immediately. Start with making Pillar content and transfer it, when you get settled with it, at that point gradually start executing Macro and Micro content. Tolerance is the key.

On the other hand that you need to be increasingly effective in creating content, you should grow better altering abilities. In the following part, we'll perceive how you can improve your altering aptitudes.

Editing your way in

Pillar Content strategy is extraordinary. It's effective and I accept each content maker must execute it. It is an expertise you should ace, and likewise with each aptitude, it'll require some investment, the more you do it, the better you'll move toward becoming at it.

Altering is the most repetitive piece of content creation. There have been times where I have invested more energy altering a video than shooting it, and I am certain it has happened to various other content makers. So for what reason does altering take so a lot of time? At the point when you are new to making content, you commit errors. It's only one out of every odd day that you sit before the camera discussing an irregular point. So you should commit errors, and to address these mix-ups, you need to watch what you've recorded. Let's assume you are making a video 'on the best way to purchase your first Digital Camera'. You shoot it, and now you get a 25-minute video. Presently, for you to alter it, you should cautiously watch this video in full, while halting and making changes any place important, and at that point approving these progressions over and over. So now it'll take you in any event 80 to an hour and a half to alter the video for a transfer.

All in all, is there a workaround for this monotonous procedure? No, shockingly there isn't. Be that as it may, as you show signs of improvement at it, you commit less errors in the pre-altering stage. Allow me to clarify; when you alter your content, you understand a portion of the things you are fouling up. You may not be taking a gander at the camera, you may state too much 'ahhs' and 'umms' when you talk, or you may articulate a word wrong. So when you see these missteps while altering, you make a mental note not to rehash them, so whenever you record a video, there'll be less botches. At the point when you've altered a great deal of content, you'll arrive at a point where you'll record better recordings/content, and as you'll be increasingly acquainted with altering, you'll complete it rapidly. So no, there isn't a workaround for altering. It is a basic advance for you to improve as a content maker.

Note: I don't recommend you re-appropriate your altering except if you truly don't possess the energy for it. As you found in the above section, it is significant that you alter your own content.

The Twitter Dilemma

In the event that you see, I have inadequately referenced Twitter in the Pillar Content strategy area, even in spite of the fact that I requested that you make a record on it at the outset. At the hour of composing this book, Twitter is practically dead. Its clients are not as dynamic as they used to be, and the measure of new Twitter clients has dove in the course of the most recent couple of years. So for what reason did I request that you make a Twitter represent your blog? All things considered, there are a bunch of reasons why, however first let me talk about what makes Twitter stand apart from other social media stages.

At the point when Twitter propelled in the late 2000s, individuals received the stage rapidly and it soon turned into the fury among twenty to thirty year olds. Twitter represented an alternate test for its clients, as all you have are 160 characters for every Tweet (message), and this very challenge is one reason why the stage was a gigantic achievement. Individuals grasped the test, and it was fun attempting to press a message in 160 characters, and also, emojis (emoji's) turned out to be enormously well known as they passed on additional in less character.

There is another motivation behind why Twitter picked up prominence and that is its Instantaneousness. Tweets are messages that are communicated to a crowd of people in an occasion. As far as possible is set to 160, it brings about shorter messages, which the majority of the group of spectators likes. So Twitter has continuously been the best stage to offer snappy updates to a crowd of people.

Give me a chance to give you a model: Say your preferred football crews are playing a match, which starts in a little ways from now. You switch on the Sports channel and trust that the match will start. Twenty minutes have passed, yet the match hasn't begun at this point. As of right now, what can you do to know why the match isn't going on? You'll most likely quest the Internet for an update yet you won't view much on the grounds that the occasion is as too soon to be secured by an article or be refreshed on a site.

One spot where you'll know the purpose behind the match postponement is Twitter. Either the football group's authentic record or a football devotee will have joke the purpose behind the postponement. Here is the place the Instantaneousness of Twitter proves to be useful.

You can incorporate Twitter in the Pillar content strategy, and send tweets advancing content on different stages however to get the best out of Twitter, use it as it's intended to be, Instantaneous. On the other hand that your blog specialty identifies with live sports or occasions, at that point you can offer a steady stream of updates with Twitter. Or on the other hand when you need to remark on the most recent news in your specialty, Twitter is your first go-to stage. You have to make sense of the Instantaneous piece of your specialty and use Twitter to augment it.

Truly, Twitter isn't drifting as it once used to be, yet it offers an exceptional reaction that other stages don't, and when you exploit that, you'll increase a ton of consideration.

Marketing the Content

Indeed, making content that offers some benefit isn't sufficient. You should realize how to advertise it as well. You could create the best YouTube video the world has ever observed, yet transferring it on the stage isn't sufficient. You should tell individuals that it exists. Likewise, regardless of whether you've transferred Pillar, Macro and Micro content on the stages, you'll need to advertise it.

Do you ever check the spam organizer of your email account? Only for interest, I'd ask you to look at it at the present time. All in all, what do you see?

You'll see messages for irregular limits, trick offers, and not to overlook the Nigerian Prince tricks. For what reason do you think these messages were delegated spam? Forgetting about the details, the explanation they made the spam rundown is that they don't offer any setting before their attempt to sell something.

Envision somebody coming up to you and pushing items in your face, encouraging you to purchase them. Only an arbitrary more unusual moving toward you all of a sudden and attempting to sell you the most irregular stuff, how'd that make you feel? You'll be irritated and also, you don't indeed, even need to perceive what they're selling regardless of whether it was something that you should seriously mull over purchasing.

The individual in the above model is a Spammer. Regardless of whether they are attempting to sell items or market content, they constantly will in general come up short on any setting before they make their business/promoting pitch. You would prefer not to be this individual. I realize you have placed endeavors into making your content however remarking on all gateways imaginable on how individuals should look at your content isn't the best approach. You should offer setting before you request that individuals devour your content.

Setting is offering some benefit forthright which gives the peruse a feeling of your expert in the specialty which at that point makes them bound to expend your content, if you somehow managed to guide them to it.

Providing Context through Comments

Every social medium stage has a remark choice. Presently it's your opportunity to utilize this remark alternative to direct people to your blog gateways.

So search for records/directs in your specialty and afterward look at their content, attempt to offer esteem by remarking on it. For instance, in the event that I am a movement blogger, I'll search for different blogs in the travel specialty and look at their content. Suppose I discover a YouTube video titled '10 spots you need to visit on the other hand that you are arranging an outing to Europe'. Presently the video is all around made, yet as indicated by me; it needs 2-3 places that ought to have been referenced.

So I post a remark proposing 'That is one hell of a rundown you have there. I am very brave to include however.

1. Santorini, Greece: Probably the best nightfall see in the whole nation of Greece, and did I notice it has a functioning fountain of liquid magma. This island is best observed by foot and you'll likely perceive a scarcely any Bollywood melodies that were shot there.

Note: There is no Uber/Lyft in Santorini, so it's ideal to lease a sulked on the other hand that you aren't 'vacating' with your squad.

2. Athens, Greece: If you have seen any of the Hollywood motion pictures spinning around the Greek domain, at that point you should see Athens. The fifth century Parthenon sanctuary made for the goddess of intelligence, Athena will make you wonder about the Grandeur of the Greek realm. It might look fundamental from the photos; however it is striking to

watch it face to face. I suggest booking your tickets online as that may spare you long stretches of remaining in a line at the doors.

On the other hand that you watch the above remark, I didn't make reference to that I am a movement blogger. For what reason did I do that? All things considered, the first and the main go for my remark was to offer extraordinary worth, which I did. Posting two significant places in Europe and giving pivotal transportation tips is an extraordinary piece of guidance for movement fans. What's more, the individuals who discover my recommendation important will look at my profile/channel without a doubt, and some of them will buy in to the equivalent. Not referencing my blog in any way makes me look less edgy for a group of people and makes me go over an individual who is exclusively keen on offering some incentive, an ideal counterpart for content customers.

The above strategy applies over every single social medium stage, so it relies upon you, how much you will be you ready to utilize it and on what number of stages? My recommendation is blend it up between the stages.

The world well known Marketing Guru Gary Vaynerchuk a.k.a Gary Vee presented a strategy called as the '$1.80 strategy', which includes leaving your input (esteem) on 90 events for every day. He says that makers like you and me should remark in any event 90 times each day to increment their range and the brand. Mind you, he isn't looking at spamming 90 remarks, rather offering some benefit with your remark multiple times in a day.

Presently to individuals understanding this, remarking multiple times in a day may sound simple yet trust me, it isn't. Duplicate gluing a line that says, 'Hello, I produce Gaming recordings on my channel, look at it' is simple and anybody can do it. Be that as it may, composing something valuable and astute can be saddling. So I'd prescribe you to begin moderate, possibly with a point of 5-10 remarks for every day, and bit by bit increment the recurrence as you improve at it. Keep in mind however, the quality ought to stay flawless, don't attempt to arrive at the 50 remark mark by hurrying through 40 of them.

Be a Quora Sherlock

On the other hand that you haven't knew about the inquiry and-answer site 'Quora' at that point you better acclimate with it since we'll be utilizing it a great deal. Quora is easy to utilize, individuals pose inquiries, and other individuals attempt to answer them in the most ideal manner conceivable. So how does a blogger like you take bit of leeway of Quora? Here's the ticket:

Inquiries on Quora are sorted. So you can peruse questions dependent on a specific point, you can look for inquiries that spin around your blog specialty. When you find significant questions, attempt to answer them as well as could be expected and yet, direct the group of spectators to your blog gateways, and here's the way you can do that:

Initially, pursue a record on Quora. Ensure you include your blog and different gateways in the accreditations. When done, search for inquiries in your specialty. These inquiries will go from very essential to unmistakable. I'd encourage you to answer the essential ones first. The key here is to answer the question and after that end the appropriate response with something like:"

I regularly talk about subjects like these on my blog. Look at it:

Blog Website: abc.com

YouTube: www.youtube.com/abc

Facebook: www.facebook.com/abc

Instagram: www.instagram.com/abc

Sometimes the inquiries will be on a theme you've canvassed in a blog post, this is the opportunity to compose a short form of that post as the appropriate response and include an entry, for example, 'This is a selection from my blog post. Look at the full form here: I've likewise made a video on the equivalent, check it around here:'

You should realize that not just the individuals who've posed the inquiry will see your answer, however different guests will likewise observe it. Truth be told, on the other hand that you scan for an inquiry on Google, you are almost certain to see a Quora answer in the main three outcomes. Thus, on the other hand that you are reliable with your answers on Quora, you can guide a huge amount of traffic to your blog entries.

On the other hand that you watch, the way to expanding your group of spectators base is to offer enough an incentive to a guest for them to consider you as somebody who realizes the specialty superior to them. When you accomplish that, at that point individuals will need to tail you, independent of the vehicle of content.

Paid Social Media Advertising

I exhorted you to remark on social media, attempt to offer your feedback on things however there is an underutilized side of social media which can enable you to earn a great deal of traffic: Paid Advertising. Before you scrutinize me for not being quiet and everything, let me explain my line of reasoning.

Have you at any point thought about how social media stages profit? You get everything for nothing on Facebook, YouTube, and different stages, so how would they get paid? Indeed, let me start by a adage during the 1970s on TV publicizing, 'In case you're not paying for the item, you are the item'. What the majority of the individuals utilizing social media don't comprehend is these stages profit. How precisely? Allows find to out.

I'll begin with a model. Let's assume you headed out to watch a motion picture with your buddies. At the cinema, you click an image with your companions and post it on Facebook. In the post, you notice the cinema and the name of the motion picture. State the film was 'Vindicators: End Game'.

Jump to one week from now, you are looking through your feed, and you unearth an advertisement for a T-shirt gathering themed on the most recent Avengers motion picture. Incident? I think not. Upon the arrival of the motion picture, you posted your area and the film name on Facebook. Presently, Facebook gathers this data and spares it to a document that has the various data you've posted up until this point. This data is then used to frame a character profile of you which shows qualities as what you might possibly like yet more significantly; it shows what you could conceivably purchase.

Each time you post on social media, the information gets gathered and added as parameters to refine this profile of yours. You may have as of late posted your new bicycle picture while labeling the producer, this information at that point gets gathered and handled and now the social media stage realizes that you are keen on bicycles and you've as of late purchased another bicycle from a explicit maker. Let's assume you visit an Amusement park with your family, and snap a couple photographs and transfer them on Instagram. Presently Instagram will utilize these transferred photographs to refine your profile by including Amusement Parks as one of your inclinations.

So for what reason do social media stages do this? Is it accurate to say that it isn't control? In the advertising scene, a directed rundown of individuals is outright gold. Let's assume you claim a vehicle business in the place where you grew up, and on an irregular day, you jump on the top of your store, get a Megaphone out and continue saying, "Vehicles!! Anybody need vehicles! We have a ton of them". I'd state you'd catch a great deal of eye however for all an inappropriate reasons, and also, it won't really enable you to sell autos. State seven days afterward, a man visits your store and makes you an offer. He says, "Sir, I can get you a rundown of individuals living in this town that are hoping to purchase a vehicle at the present time, with their personal residence and telephone numbers". Suspicious from the start, you'd guide him to get the rundown and after that you'll make an arrangement. The person says, "Okay", and leaves just to return two days after the fact with a rundown in his grasp.

He gives you the rundown and says, "This rundown contains the names, locations and telephone numbers of the considerable number of individuals in this town who need to purchase a vehicle immediately". In the wake of approving the rundown, you hand the person an attractive heap of money saying, "We'd like to work with you once more". As point by point as that story seemed to be, there is a moment takeaway here, the person gave you a rundown of individuals hoping to purchase a vehicle, so if you somehow managed to approach these individuals, doubtlessly they'd purchase from your business. You paid the person abundantly in light of the fact that he gave you a focused on rundown of potential clients, which is gold for your business.

Essentially, in the showcasing scene, directed group of spectators is gold, and that is actually what social media stages offer to the advertisers. For what reason do you think you just get indicated advertisements that you are inspired by? Social media stages sell promoting space and yet offer the advertisers the capacity to demonstrate their promotions just to a specific statistic with explicit qualities, which results in a superior active visitor clicking percentage which at that point brings about better deals.

Keep in mind when I stated, I don't care for social media much? All things considered, this is one of the key purposes behind it. Things being what they are, are social media stages beguiling you? Not in essence. You willfully put the data out there; the stages don't constrain you to do it. Is it reasonable on an ethical level? No, yet since when did enormous organizations care about ethical quality? I am making an effort not to denounce social media stages; I simply need you to realize that they are no holy people either. With above models, I needed to represent how social media stages gather information. As a content maker, you should utilize social media to showcase your content to the correct group of spectators. I realize I sound like a go getter after my tirade on social media however what will be will be, and each blogger's group of spectators exists on social media, so why not receive the best in return?

So I don't get my meaning by receiving the best in return? All things considered, as I've represented above, when you promote on social media stages, you can target group of spectators with explicit attributes,

and that is what we will do to showcase our content.
So what content would it be a good idea for you to
showcase? How can one go about this? You can
either advertise your content for presentation or you
can have a go at something I like to call 'Deft
Marketing'. Allow me to expand.

Let's assume you are a photography blogger. You've
posted a couple of recordings on inclining themes
however there is one specific video titled 'When
should you put resources into a DSLR Camera' that
you accept is your best work. The video gets
predictable perspectives, yet is no chance to get close
to what it merits. Here is where you can actualize
paid Social Media Advertising for the video. What
will you get in return? Indeed, in the event that your
video offers extraordinary worth, at that point you
and your channel will get heaps of consideration and

a great deal of supporters. The above model outlines utilizing paid Social Media Promoting for presentation.

The other method for utilizing paid Social Media Advertising expects you to be an Opportunist.

Give me a chance to give you an individual model, I began blogging as a Tech blogger, and toward the start of my voyage, I didn't have quite a bit of an after to keep in touch with home about however I was acknowledged as an subsidiary for Amazon. So one day, I got messages from the Amazon Affiliate group in regards to an electronic deal occurring in seven days' time on Amazon. I had recently perused some paid Social Media Promoting articles, so I thought this was the ideal open door for me to attempt it. So I concocted a plan for it and here is the means by which it went:

It was a three-day deal and it would be live in five days. So I utilized those five days to get ready for it by composing a no frills form of content for the deal. I composed content posts, for example, '5 best arrangements of the Amazon Electronic Sale', 'Best Earphones you can purchase during the Amazon Electronic Sale', and so forth., yet I didn't transfer them. I didn't have the foggiest idea about the arrangements, so there was no reason for transferring the posts on the blog however I made the pages, gave them a title and dealt with the easily overlooked details. All I required was, the deal to start. The deal was to start at 12 PM, when it begun, I experienced the arrangements and composed the content, included associate connections any place fundamental and I was finished. I have a great deal of involvement in the innovation field, so posting items weren't troublesome and in around two hours, my content was fit to be distributed.

I distributed the content on the blog and went to Facebook. I had a Facebook page for the blog where I composed a post with the title 'The Best Deals from the Amazon Electronic Sale', included the blog page interface and booked the post for 3-day Facebook advancement. I focused on the post to Facebook clients who had 'electronic contraptions' and 'cell phones' as interests. The paid advancement cost me around $50

For the three-day electronic deal, my Ad was on the feed of individuals keen on electronic contraptions and cell phones. After the deal, I checked the insights of the advancement and to my shock I surpassed my desires. The advanced posts brought over a thousand ticks, of which, near 50 requests were made, where I made a partner commission of $200. I had contributed about $50 on Facebook Advertising, and I received $200 consequently. So I made a benefit of $150. Not terrible for a beginner!

I know $150 may not seem like a major ordeal to you, however I simply needed to represent the potential of Social Media Advertising for your content. The fact of the matter isn't to trick your supporters into purchasing ambiguous items in light of a deal. You have to give out your legit sentiments about these items, and if the guest chooses to get it, you are offering them an immediate connection.

In the event that you are going to actualize something like this, recollect to not get drawn into it. On the other hand that a item gives you 10% as associate commission yet it isn't extraordinary, at that point there is no point suggesting it. Have honesty; if an item gives you no subsidiary commission by any means, yet is a incredible item, at that point you ought to suggest it. Try not to pursue the brisk buck, have tolerance and you'll get what you merit.

Not every single social medium stage can give you the best outcomes for paid publicizing. Be cautious where you promote. Facebook and Instagram are the best stages for Social Media Promoting at the present time, they offer much more reach at a less expensive cost. On the other hand that your content is more visual, contains recordings or photographs, at that point you can never turn out badly with Instagram. At the hour of composing this book, Instagram is the most sweltering social media stage, so benefit as much as possible from it while it keeps going.

Try not to put resources into Twitter Ads by any stretch of the imagination; Twitter is practically out of

Buzz. It can skip back for all we know, yet when and in the event that it does, you'll know it. For the present, Twitter Ads are costly and try not to offer enough reach. Avoid them.

Social Media Advertising can be extraordinary just whenever utilized appropriately. So if an open door presents itself in your specialty, a little venture into promoting will present to you a great deal of significant worth.

The Elusive Email List

An email-list is a rundown of email locations of individuals keen on your content or specialty. Bloggers use email-records to convey advancements for new content, offers, alliance arrangements and the sky is the limit from there. So how would you get an email-list and do you really require one?

We're in 2019, and you'd think we are finished with all types of E-mail promoting at this point and there is no reason for putting cash or time into it, however hang on a second! Email is as yet one of the most ideal approaches to market content on the Internet. Indeed, social media has never been more famous, yet email still holds its ground and I trust it will continue holding it. So for what reason is it so? Social media stages offer every one of the highlights you need, so for what reason do we keep effectively utilizing our email accounts?

The appropriate response is less difficult than you may might suspect. Individuals have consistently thought of email as a more individual and formal method of correspondence. Corporate representatives still use email for major affirmations and formal solicitations. You get all the significant budgetary affirmations/notices by means of email. Truly, we get more spam messages than previously, yet that has never made us leave the email environment.

May be it has to do with email driving the way when the Internet upheaval started and individuals picking into it from the beginning. There is this feeling of wellbeing with email that individuals don't find anyplace else. When you book a flight ticket, where do you get the affirmation? Email. Made an enormous exchange, where do you get the receipt? Email. Going after a position or entry level position, where do you get the affirmation? Email.

How frequently do you browse your messages? I am speculating least once every day, and like you, the greater part of the individuals online browses their messages in any event once per day. Would you be able to state the equivalent for social media? No. Leave aside social media clients matured 15-24, and it leaves you with a greater part of individuals who don't check their social media stages each day. So overall, you are more prone to answer to an email than a Facebook post. Presently, as a blogger, how might you take preferred position of the email stage to advertise your content? Allow's find to out.

Each guest to your blog is here and there or other keen on content of your specialty, that is why they've visited the blog in any case. Or then again perhaps they are lost, which is profoundly impossible. So if you somehow happened to elevate your content to your blog guests, they are probably going to interface with it in some shape or structure. To elevate your content to your blog guests, you have to get their email address. Be that as it may, in this time of Spam sends and Nigerian sovereign cases how does a blogger get this tricky email address? All things considered, you can't simply request it; perhaps 10 years back it could have worked however not presently. You have to offer a motivation.

Has it at any point transpired where you visit a blog and as you are going to leave you get a spring up window which says something like, "Get my master class eBook on 'run' for totally Has it at any point transpired where you visit a blog and as you are going to leave you get a spring up window which says something like, "Get my master class eBook on 'run' for totally.

How about we discover how you can construct an email list for your blog utilizing a motivating force.

Allows first make our impetus. You have to make a Digital item that individuals need to expend, preferably in a book structure, however can be a video or a sound. The Digital item can be a 10 page pdf, a five to ten-minute video or a sound, as long as it gives enough an incentive to lure the guest into giving their email address.

Consider something essential, in the event that you are an innovation blogger, at that point a 15 page (3K-5K words) eBook that advises the peruse how to purchase their next cell phone is an extraordinary Digital item to utilize. Or on the other hand if you are a movement blogger, at that point an eBook on '10 things each movement lover should claim' sounds incredible. A short eBook is simpler to compose, however on the other hand that you have a short video or sound that gives incredible worth, at that point put it all on the line. You could transfer the video on YouTube, make it private, what's more, share the connection as a motivating force, which is greatly improved than giving individuals a huge video document to download.

There isn't a need to go all extravagant on the item, compose the vital material, give a little introduction and an outro, and you are finished. You don't have to compose new material for the item, you can experience your prior blog posts and concentrate key focuses, aggregate them and you have an extraordinary Digital item to offer.

The Internet group of spectators is progressively mindful presently, so chances are, a large portion of them realize that you are looking for their email addresses, which are still fine; we're not perpetrating a wrongdoing here. This is where I return to the point of making a compelling Digital item. Regardless of whether they know you need their email address, the item should make them offer it to you.

When you have a Digital item to offer, presently it's an ideal opportunity to utilize an email promoting instrument to take care of the conveyance procedure. 'Mail Chimp' is one of the most famous promoting instruments in the world, and above all, it offers a free arrangement where you can utilize the administration to gather, keep up, and provide food for up to 2000 contacts (email addresses). In this way, make a record on Mail Chimp and select in to the free arrangement.

When your blog traffic develops, at that point you can consider moving up to a paid arrangement. Mail Chimp has an easy to understand interface, which encourages you structure messages, join structures and significantly more. So plan a sign-up structure on Mail chimp, add it to your blog site, and start fabricating your email list.

When you have an email list, keep up it by giving steady worth. When possibly 14 days, send a bulletin to your email list which features late content on the blog. Try not to send them the entire post, separate key focuses from your posts, and send them with a connect to the unique post. Start simple. On the other hand that you can just make one bit of content for each week, that is fine, gathering the content like clockwork, infer key focuses and send them in the pamphlet. A month to month pamphlet fills in also, as long as it offers some benefit.

An email rundown resembles giving a dough puncher a rundown of the entire close by individuals who expend pastry kitchen items, the dough puncher can straightforwardly promote to the mass and get various deals. An email list gives you the chance to market to a focused on crowd yet use it admirably. On the other hand that you keep spamming your email list with special messages each other day, they will withdraw to your messages, and that is one of the most noticeably awful things that can happen to a blogger. With incredible power comes extraordinary obligation!

The vast majority approve of accepting one email for each week. Regardless of whether they aren't keen on the content, they won't be withdrawing to you at any point in the near future. Try not to test their resilience however. An email list with 200 passages and a 80% open rate (normal of the quantity of individuals who tapped on the email to open it) is superior to anything a 1000 passage email list with a 10% open rate, since regardless of whether a hundred people opened the email for the last case, the sheer open rate is low, and it'll continue corrupting further. Treat your email rundown like gold.

Summary

Blogging is a great voyage that warrants Self-Discovery and Expression. The Internet has leveled the field by giving equivalent voice to everybody included; ensure you utilize yours to the best of your capacity. Keep in mind; each time you accept the open door to convey what needs be, you are opening the entryway for analysis however absolutely never let it trouble you. In the first place, you'll have so a lot to state yet not many ready to tune in and that is the point at which you should keep your confidence and continue pushing ahead. In this on edge world, is the patient one!

I expectation you've taken in something important from this book. My plan for composing this book was to furnish you with an essential diary that never gets old. In the event that you ever experience an issue on your blogging venture, don't hesitate to connect with me. My contact data is in the 'About the Author' segment of this book. What's more, make sure to commit errors, supposing that it weren't from every one of the missteps that I did, this book would have never occurred. Good health!!